I0755874

CONTENTS

INTRODUCTORY

LECTURE I

LECTURE II

LECTURE III

LECTURE IV

The Significance of Early Christian Eschatology

INTRODUCTORY

THE SIGNIFICANCE OF EARLY CHRISTIAN ESCHATOLOGY

ESCHATOLOGY was not so long ago the last chapter of dogmatics. The Biblical scholar was quite satisfied when he had made all the New Testament sayings about the last things fit into his system. Nobody cared what the early Christians felt and thought in reading these sayings, and but few people were personally interested in their contents. Time went on, and New Testament exegesis became historical instead of dogmatic. Students learned to ask what the

New Testament authors meant and felt. But there was so little appreciation for eschatological ideas that these were, if not neglected altogether, softened down and modernised.

It is only within the last thirty years that the attitude of Biblical theology has changed. Modern criticism allows a special interest in everything which is alien to our own time. Hence, together with angelology and demonology, eschatology to-day forms the most attractive of New Testament studies. And, as it generally happens, where there was once utter neglect, the tendency is now towards the opposite extreme—an over-estimation of the significance of eschatology on the part of a considerable number of scholars.

Under these circumstances I may be justified in laying before this distinguished assembly this question: What was the real significance of eschatology in the earliest days of Christianity?

I do not propose to deal here with early Christian eschatological doctrines in general. It is well known what a number of apocalyptic ideas were current during that period. We may take it for granted that all these were borrowed from Judaism, whatever may have been their origin. The gospel introduced two new points only: (1) the central place was given to Jesus, whose parousia or descent from heaven in the glory of the Father was to bring with it the end of this world, the resurrection, the judgment, the kingdom of God, and life everlasting; and (2) this was expected to happen very speedily, the Messiah having been sent already by God in the person of Jesus, and being postponed for a short space only. This is the vital point: early Christianity was not simply meditating on eschatological dreams that might be realised some time or other at a remote period, but the first Christians were persuaded that the great day when all would be changed was to come in the lifetime of their own generation.

No modern scholar will deny, I trust, that Jesus Himself and His disciples, including the Apostle Paul, shared this persuasion. Of course, it cannot be proved that Jesus ever thought that He would succeed in establishing the kingdom of God without dying first. It is a widespread hypothesis among scholars of our time that He did so, at least in the first period of His ministry; that He tried to win His people by preaching and healing, and that He was only led by the experience of growing hatred on the part of His countrymen to reckon, first with the possibility, then with the necessity, of His death, and, finally, to attribute to it a positive efficacy. In vain we ask for proofs of this theory. Jesus says that unto this (present) generation no sign should be given,[1] that there were some of them that stood there who should not taste of death till they had seen the kingdom of God come with power.[2] He never speaks of His own lifetime[3]; it is only in the next generation that the kingdom will come. His disciples have to wait for it, as they pray for its coming.[4]

And thus the apostles, when Jesus was taken from them, taught the people that Jesus of Nazareth, whom the chiefs of the Jews put to death, was the man ordained

1 Mark viii. 12. 2 Mark ix. 9.

3 Matt. x. 23 is to be understood of the missionary work after Jesus's death, not of the disciples' short trip through Galilee.

4 Matt. vi. 10.

by God; but they did not tell them that the new era had already begun. The kingdom was still to be expected. Jesus must come back from heaven to establish it, and would come quickly.

St. Paul felt sure that he would be still alive at the coming. "We which are alive and remain," he says to the Thessalonians[1]; and in his first letter to the Corinthians he expresses the same view.[2] Later on his attitude changes. As a matter of fact, in the second to the Corinthians, his position has become uncertain; still he hopes and wishes that death may not come to him before Christ's parousia; but having realised that death can come suddenly, even upon him, he declares solemnly his confidence that he will be in communion with Christ even in death:

[1] 1 Thess. iv. 15, 17. [2] 1 Cor. xv. 51, 52.

"We are confident, I say, and willing rather to be absent from the body and to be present with the Lord."[1] Here we find for the first time the individual death taking the place of the parousia, an alternative often suggested by later Christian writers. But Paul does not at all mean to set aside the enthusiastic expectation of Christ's immediate advent. His only doubt is this: will he himself be still alive? The event is not postponed; on the contrary, it draws nigh rapidly, as he writes to the Romans: "Now is our salvation nearer than when we believed."[2] And even in the last of his letters he declares: "We look for the salvation from heaven."[3]

To these testimonies we may add the opening and the closing words of St. John's Revelation: "Things which must

[1] 2 Cor. v. 6–8. [2] Rom. xiii. 11–12.
[3] Phil. iii. 20.

shortly come to pass;" "For the time is at hand;" "Surely I come quickly. Amen. Even so, Lord Jesus".[1] It is impossible not to see how deeply early Christianity was impressed with this conviction.

Not a single modern scholar, I feel sure, will deny these statements. The question, however, is how far this belief in an immediate coming of the end acted upon the mind of Jesus and of His disciples. We shall find that it did not do so as much as we might expect.

Jesus declares that the gospel must be preached to all nations before the kingdom can come;[2] but He does not go beyond the Jewish frontiers.[3] Although at the sending out of His disciples to preach in the cities and villages of Palestine His

[1] Rev. i. 1, 3; xxii. 20.

[2] Mark xiii. 10.

[3] Mark vi. 1 ff.

orders show that He would have them hurry on,[1] He Himself makes no haste at all. There is no evidence that He ever dreamt of hastening on the day of the Lord by His activity or His suffering, that (to quote from a recent author) He was possessed with the idea that His intervention would bring to a standstill the wheel of history.

And even St. Paul, much as he was impressed by the urgent need of accomplishing his missionary work throughout the world before the coming of Christ,[2] did not hurry on from town to town ; on the contrary, he was anxious to stay as long as his activity was needed, not merely to found, but to develop and to educate a Christian community.

Now, as a matter of fact, in his exhor-

[1] Mark vi. 8–12. [2] Rom. xv. 16.

tation he frequently insists on the approach of judgment and final salvation.[1] When he appeals to scriptural "examples" he justifies himself by the remark that the end of the time has come upon his readers.[2] But we cannot say that this view materially influenced his ethics. Many scholars maintain that we have to explain from the eschatological point of view what Paul says about marriage in 1 Cor. vii., and, indeed, his general idea is that, as the time is short, nothing should be changed; he who was married when he became a Christian should remain married; he who was unmarried should so remain: "let every man abide in the same calling wherein he was called."[3] His preference for celibacy, however, is not to be explained by his

[1] 1 Thess. v. 1 ff.; Rom. xii. 11.

[2] 1 Cor. x. 11.

[3] 1 Cor. vii. 17, 20, 24.

eschatology[1]; it was the asceticism of his age which influenced him in regarding marriage as the lower state.

Jesus certainly looks forward to a rich harvest, which is to be given to the poor, the hungry, the merciful, the pure in heart,[2] and so on, when the kingdom comes; and this will be very soon. He insists on the duty of being watchful, because the day will come suddenly as a thief in the night.[3] But if we eliminate His eschatological ideas His ethics remain unchanged. Take, for example, the parables of the Good Samaritan and of the Prodigal Son.[4] The great commandments of love

[1] 1 Cor. vii. 26, 31, have been partly misinterpreted, partly overvalued in their significance.

[2] Matt. v. 3–12; Luke vi. 20–22.

[3] Matt. xxiv. 42–44.

[4] Luke x. 30 ff.; xv. 11 ff.

and of self-renunciation[1] are in no way suggestive of an "interim ethics," but of a definite, absolute system of ethics.

And in this way His ethical precepts were understood, taught, and acted upon by the early Christians.[2] That they are strange to our modern Christian mind is not due to the fact that we have abandoned the eschatological idea, but to the fact that the enthusiasm which inspired them and made their fulfilment easy is no longer ours. This enthusiasm, however, has its roots not so much in eschatology as in the profound consciousness of a change already accomplished through the experience of salvation, as we shall see hereafter.

It is true that neither Jesus nor Paul

[1] Mark xii. 28–34; Matt. v. 38–48; Luke vi. 26, 27.

[2] *E.g.*, 1 Thess. v. 15; Rom. xii. 17–21.

conceived the idea of a gradual development of the kingdom, or of an extension of the Church through a long period of history upon earth. Jesus's first coming was not indeed the end, but at the end of history. It is from this point of view that we have to understand what Jesus Himself says about His death, as a ransom for many and the making of a new covenant.[1] He looks backward in history. The new covenant will be in another æon, not on this earth, not under these conditions of life.[2] When St. Paul speaks of Jesus as a propitiation, and of the redemption and forgiveness of all sins by His death,[3] this is intelligible on the supposition that what stands at the end of history extends its influence backwards

[1] Mark x. 45; xiv. 24.

[2] Mark xii. 25; xiv. 25.

[3] Rom. iii. 25.

upon the whole period which preceded. Paul does not think about the sins of millions of men, who will live after Christ's death. When he insists on the parallelism between Adam and Christ,[1] he is thinking of humanity in its beginning and in its end. Christ is not the centre or turning-point of a great historical development, as we may now call Him from our remote standpoint, but He is the end itself. What follows is no continuation, but a renovation of what has gone before, a new humanity in a new world.

Thus the general conception of history in primitive Christianity so characteristic of Jewish thought as contrasted with Greek philosophy is strongly influenced by what we may call the eschatological idea. And it is this historical conception which

[1] Rom. v. 12–21.

throws light upon the early Christian theories of redemption.

These theories, however, are but a form of religious thought, just as ethics are only a way of forming the moral power of Christendom. When we ask what is the kernel of early Christian religious feeling, we shall find that there is nothing eschatological about it.

Jesus's religious position may be rightly defined as a life of unbroken union with God. The Judaism of His time, even in its most pious form, thought of God as of a distant Being, removed and completely separated from this world of sin, which was given into the dominion of subordinate or even evil spirits until the time when God should come to judge the world and to establish His own sovereignty. Jesus knows Him—and teaches men to know Him—as the Father, who, always and everywhere present, cares about the welfare of all His children;[1] who has compassion on the sinner and forgives trespasses whenever man repents. It is in the strength of this trust that Jesus goes on His way, undisturbed by hostile threats;[2] that He sleeps in the storm,[3] feeds the multitude,[4] heals all kinds of sickness,[5] and casts out the demons.[6] Thence He gets a conception of the *βασιλεία τού θεοῦ* quite different from the current one; the kingdom of God is not to be brought about by a miraculous act of God, but it is the domination of God casting away all evil powers.[7] Jesus

[1] Matt. v. 45; Luke vi. 35.

[2] Luke xiii. 31, 32.

[3] Mark iv. 37–40.

[4] Mark vi. 34–40; viii. 13–26.

[5] Mark i. 32 ff.; ii. 5; v. 34; xi. 23, 24.

[6] Mark iii. 22 ff.

[7] Matt. xii. 28; Luke xi. 20. Cp. Luke x. 18.

Himself by His complete union with God brings in this domination of God: it is where *He* is; it is present among men; it is to be found in men's hearts, and not to be looked for in external miraculous signs.[1] So Jesus—in His own opinion—is not only preparing the future kingdom of God, like His forerunner, John the Baptist, but He is actually bringing it in.[2] He is the bridegroom whose companions cannot fast while He is with them.[3] From the parables of the garment and of the wine-bottles[4] we learn that He looks on Himself and His surroundings as something quite new. He does not speak much of the new spirit, but all His acting is dominated by a new spirit. So is that

1 Luke xvii. 21.

2 Matt. xi. 9–10; Luke vii. 26–8; xvi. 16.

3 Mark ii. 19.

4 Mark ii. 21, 22; Matt. xiii. 16, 17.

of His disciples. Of course, in His addresses to the people He speaks as the missionary; there is the need to be watchful, for the great moment will come shortly, suddenly. But in the intimate circle of His followers there is no anxious self-preparation for judgment to come, but a happy enjoyment of all blessings which God's grace had vouchsafed to them in Jesus. This is the meaning of Peter's confession:[1] "People may say, Thou art a prophet, one of a large number, an Elijah or John, *i.e.*, the forerunner of a greater one. *We* confess that Thou art the Christ, the unique bringer of salvation: there is none greater than Thou; in Thee we enjoy our union with God, in short our salvation."

It is this spirit of gladness, caused by

[1] Mark viii. 28, 29.

the experience of the greatest gifts of God, that we discern in the disciples after Jesus had gone from them. Whether it be called the experience of communion with the risen Lord or the communion of the Holy Ghost, it is not the anticipation of something yet to come; it is the actual possession of a present benefit.

This fact becomes still more patent when we turn once more to St. Paul. What has the triumphant hymn in Rom. viii. to do with eschatology? The Christian is sure of God's love as shown and guaranteed to him by Christ who came down and died for this very purpose, and by the Holy Ghost, which is given into his heart.[1] Salvation is at hand, God has performed, Christ has died and risen, the Holy Ghost has been given to every

[1] Rom. v. 5–8; viii. 32.

believer. Christians, then, are washed, sanctified, justified.[1] They are living in a new state; "old things are passed away; behold, all things are become new."[2]

Eschatology, it is true, is at the background of all this, but it has changed its significance. Many sayings of Jesus and Paul are then only fully intelligible if we recognise that eschatological terms are used by them in a new sense; they discard all external, political, miraculous significance, but take the inward moral meaning as already fulfilled.[3] At the same time they do not entirely eliminate the other meaning; putting forward the new, they retain the original one combined with it. If time present had brought fulfilment, still larger fulfilment is in store for time to come.

[1] 1 Cor. vi. 11; i. 30.
[2] 2 Cor. v. 17.
[3] See, *e.g.*, 1 Cor. iv. 8.

Jesus, like all great religious personalities, was at once progressive and eminently conservative. The new gifts which He had to bring to mankind are envisaged by Himself in the form of old Jewish conceptions. External reality did not correspond to what people expected, to what Jesus Himself found in the prophets. There was still a lack of external glory. Now Jesus trusted to His Father that He would accomplish what He had begun, and fulfil all that He had promised. And so eschatology in its old form was for Him a postulate of His faith. The kingdom is at hand, it is present in His person, in His casting out devils, in His bringing sinners to repentance—but it has still to come in glory, when after His death and resurrection He will come upon the clouds from heaven.[1] Men are God's beloved

[1] Mark viii. 38 ; xiv. 62.

and happy children; so runs His message, and they are this if they are merciful even as He is.[1] But He can also say, "Blessed are the peacemakers, for they shall be called the children of God."[2] So in Jesus's preaching everything is at once present and future: you have it, you will receive it.

The same may be said of St. Paul's doctrine: there we find not only the double conception of the kingdom, present and future,[3] but also that of sonship, of redemption, of deliverance, of righteousness, and so on. We are children of God; we have the spirit of sonship, and yet we have to wait for the manifestation of the sons of God; we wait for the sonship.[4] We are redeemed, and yet we look for

[1] Matt. v. 45; Luke vi. 35. [2] Matt. v. 9.

[3] Rom. xiv. 17; 1 Cor. iv. 20; 1 Thess. ii. 12; 1 Cor. vi. 9, 10; Gal. v. 21.

[4] Rom. viii. 14, 16, 19, 23.

the redemption of our body.[1] Paul feels himself a new creature, exalted above all human misery and sin: and yet all that he now has, is but a small portion of what he will obtain when his Lord comes in His glory to glorify those who belong to Him.[2] If Christ's death has done such great things, he argues in Romans v., to reconcile us with God how great will be the effect of Christ's life,[3] *i.e.*, of His coming in glory and of our being united with Him eternally.

We are now in a better position to understand how it is that Paul, when changing his opinion as to the time of his own death in relation to the parousia, did not forthwith set aside the old conception (as we should have expected, had he been merely abandoning Rabbinical views for

[1] 1 Cor. i. 30; Rom. viii. 23.

[2] 2 Cor. v. 17.

[3] Rom. v. 9, 10.

Hellenistic ones). Even in the latest of his letters he holds both conceptions: on the one hand he can desire to depart and to be with Christ; on the other he can anticipate Christ's return from heaven to conform the body of our humiliation to the body of His glory.[1]

It would be easy to demonstrate these alternating views by the Rabbinical doctrine of the two Olams (æons, worlds), the one present, bad, evil, and the other future, glorious, happy. The New Testament writers use the terms, but it is difficult to say how precisely they view their own age. If Christ came that He might deliver us from the present evil world, Christians belong already to the new world. And yet all the external conditions of the old bad world still exist. Christians dwell still in the flesh, but they walk not after

[1] Phil. i. 20; iii. 20, 21.

the flesh; or, as St. John says, they are in the world but not of the world. It is remarkable that we nowhere find an explicit theory of an intermediate state like later doctrines of the twofold advent of Christ, or the later distinction between *ecclesia militans* and *ecclesia triumphans*. The early Christians were so enthusiastic in their belief in an accomplished salvation that, in spite of all external evidence, they imagined themselves already dwelling in the new order of things. If St. Mark illustrates the effect of Christ's death by the veil of the temple rent in twain from the top to the bottom, the Gospel according to St. Matthew anticipate the signs of the parousia and the last judgment by the earthquake, the opening of the graves, and the rise of the many bodies of the saints.[1]

[1] Mark xv. 38; Matt. xxvii. 51, 52.

This attitude of early Christianity is to be seen in its clearest form in the Johannine writings. It is well known that the fourth evangelist (whoever he may be) uses eschatological terms in the modified sense: ζωή αἰώνιος, "eternal life," is not, as in other books, the life of the æon to come, but it is something that begins in this life,—life in the highest sense—whereas what men call life is but death. So Christ gives life everlasting to all who know Him and believe in Him. So, too, judgment and resurrection are taken in a figurative sense: for the Christian judgment lies in the past; he has passed from death into life;[1] the κρίσις is effected by the separation of believers and unbelievers.[2] It is to be understood in this figurative sense when Jesus says: "The hour is coming, and now

[1] John v. 24. [2] John iii. 17–21.

is, when the dead shall hear the voice of the Son of God, and they that hear shall live": men, morally dead, by accepting the gospel get life everlasting.[1] But when, three verses further on, he says, "For the hour is coming, in the which all that are in the tombs shall hear His voice, and shall come forth; they that have done good, unto the resurrection of life, and they that have done evil, unto the resurrection of judgment" (damnation),[2] the thought is fully eschatological. It is this combination of non-eschatological plus eschatological ideas which makes the Johannine characteristic as distinct both from primitive Christian and from Gnostic views. And yet it is the very attitude of Jesus and Paul which we recognise in this Johannine two-sidedness.

[1] John v. 25. [2] John v. 28, 29.

At this point we may stop. We have found eschatology playing a great part in early Christian belief and thought, (1) as a strong motive in moral exhortation—but only one motive besides others, such as thankfulness for God's grace, care for God's honour, Christian self-respect, and so on—and not influencing Christian ethics materially; (2) as the key to the historical conception of God's working with mankind, the sending of His Son as Saviour being the end of a long history of sin. But it was not of the essence of Christian faith, this being rather confidence in a present activity of God and an already accomplished salvation.

We may accordingly affirm that Christianity did not change its essence, when the expectation of Christ's coming became fainter and eschatology fell into the rank of a doctrine of merely historical value.

The remark may be added that the great eschatological pictures come in only at a later period of early Christian literature, not in the first, but in the second generation. That the mass of Jewish apocalyptic ideas is introduced, is in itself evidence of the weakening of early Christian confidence.

And at the same time we may determine the position of the Gospel in the history of religions. All religions of that time were religions of hope. Stress was laid on the future; the present time was but for preparation. So in the mysterious cults of Hellenism, whose highest aim is to offer guarantees for other worldly happiness; so too in Judaism, whose legacy has but the aim of furnishing the happy life in the kingdom of the future. Christianity is a religion of faith, the gospel giving not only guarantees for the future life in another world, but bringing by itself confidence, peace, joy, salvation, forgiveness, righteousness—whatever man's heart yearns after.

With this it combines hope—this we must never forget. Hope is an essential feature of vivid religious feeling. But in primitive Christian piety hope takes only the second place. When at a later period, hope takes the first rank at the expense of faith, as may be seen, *e.g.*, in 1 Peter and Hebrews, this is due to the increasing influence of pre-Christian Hellenistic religion, and means a declension. Strange to say, the weakening of eschatological feeling and the other-worldly tendency are both produced by the same movement.

Now, where all stress is laid on hope, instead of on trust, joy changes into timidity, the religious stimulus once more becomes fear. So we see the Christianity of the second century creating a new system of guarantees, exactly similar to that which the mysteries of Greece had furnished: guarantees of a future salvation—a highly uncertain salvation. But wherever there is a revival of the Gospel, *e.g.*, in St. Augustine, St. Francis, Luther, and the other heroes of the Reformation, we meet again joyful confidence and assurance of salvation combined with a secure hope of still greater blessings.

This is the proof from history for our thesis.

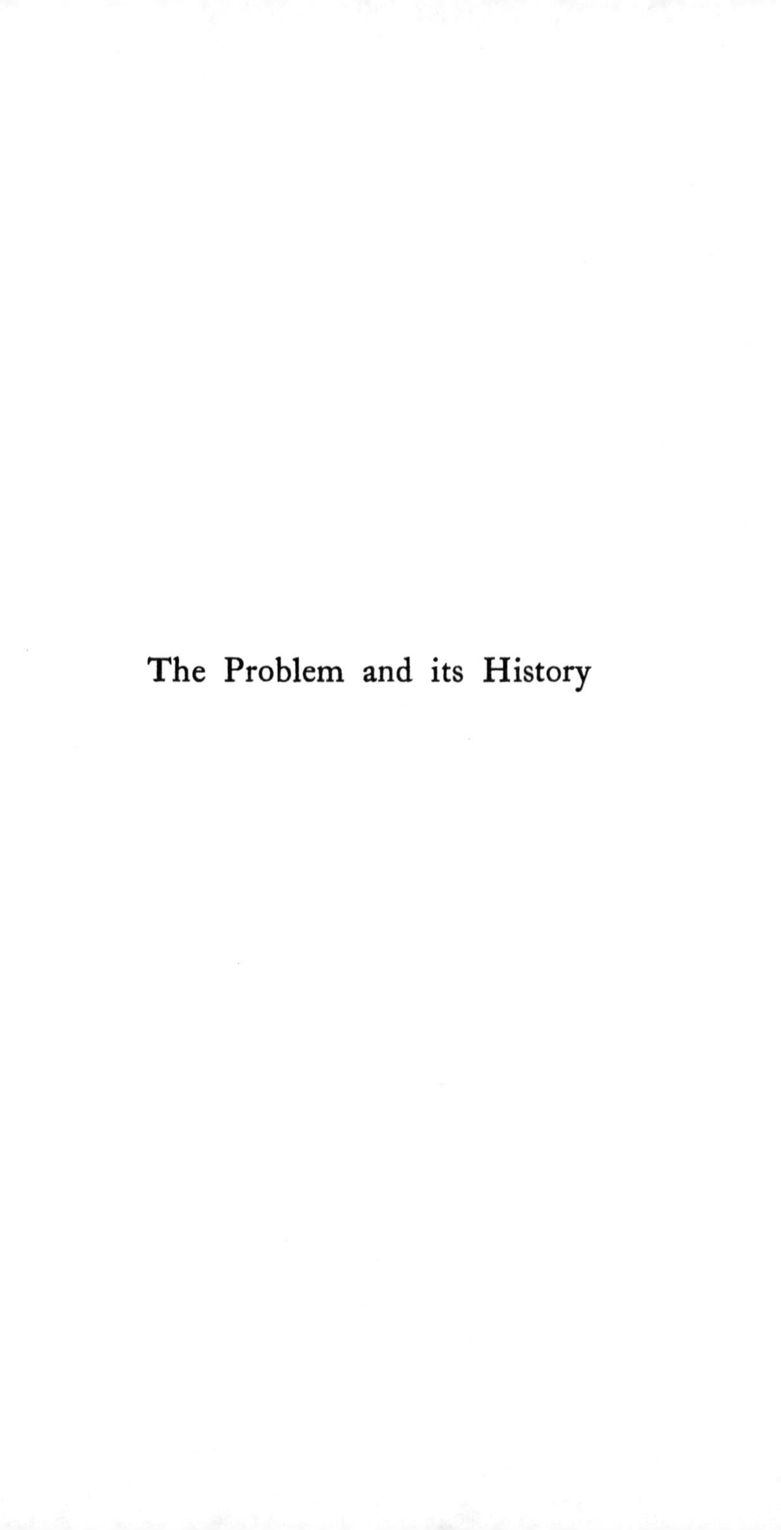

The Problem and its History

LECTURE I

THE PROBLEM AND ITS HISTORY

ESCHATOLOGY is at the present moment a favourite subject which attracts more and more the interest of large circles. I hope, therefore, that the following four lectures, which were delivered at the Summer School of Theology at Oxford, September 1909, may be welcomed here. I give them, with the exception of some slight alterations, in the original form of lectures.

The subject, as it was formulated by the Committee of the Summer School, is not equivalent to "The eschatology of

Jesus"—it includes much more; nor is it so comprehensive as the paper read before the third International Congress for the history of religions, at Oxford, September 1908, on "The Significance of early Christian eschatology."[1] As it is given, the subject places us before the whole gospel-question, reminding us of two most important points which we never should lose sight of in studying the Gospels, two points indeed which make the problem so intricate and difficult: first that all depends on "the Gospel," *i.e.* on what Jesus Himself thought and said; and secondly, that we have this only in the form of "the Gospels," *i.e.* in the different forms of tradition. Or, to use Matthew Arnold's words: "All our criticism of the four Evangelists who report Jesus has this for its governing idea: to make out what

[1] See above, p. 1–33.

in their report of Jesus is Jesus, and what is the reporters."[1]

I

Before we attack the problem itself, it will be desirable to say a few words with regard to its history. This, I think, is what a methodical study needs most. It makes the distinction between the reading of a scholar and a dilettante. The latter, when he comes across any question, will at once go into it or through it with his own brains only, and perhaps one or two books with which chance has provided him; while on the other side the scholar will, before starting, find out what the question really is: what has to be said about it when it is taken in connection with all related problems, and what has been said already by

[1] *God and the Bible*, 1875, 167.

those into whose labours he is entering. Having thus fixed as a well-trained explorer the latitude and the longitude of his own position, he may say confidently: There we are, and it is in this direction that we have to go on further.

1. Now the question laid before us is, we may safely say, as so many other questions, at the same time quite old and quite recent. It is quite old, because there was no time in Church history when Christians were not occupied by the eschatological sayings in the Bible. It is quite recent, because it was only in the last century that the question became a problem in the sense of modern historical investigation. I think it is always very useful, especially for men of our own time, who are so proud of the results of modern research, to be reminded that those problems have been felt ever since the first age, that the same observa-

tions have always been made, and that it is only the method of dealing with them, the way by which we try to solve them, which changes. It has been observed from the very beginning that in the holy Scriptures there is plenty of information about the last things, the end of the world and the glorious and happy state of a new age, about judgment and final salvation. It has been felt always with keen regret that information on these subjects is so scanty, so fragmentary, so very uncertain. Now the old method was to gather all utterances scattered through the whole book and to combine them so as to gain a systematic, self-consistent view. Biblical interpretation, as you know, from the first century down to the eighteenth was dominated by dogmatic and practical presuppositions. People did not ask what Jesus said nor what the apostles meant, but what God had to tell them by the mouth of His prophets and apostles. In this way they dealt with the eschatological utterances as with a collection of divine oracles which were to be fulfilled in their present time, and thus were to be explained by the events which just then were going on. You may read Hippolytus' commentary on the Book of Daniel, or his treatise on the Antichrist, or the fifteenth catechesis of Bishop Cyril of Jerusalem, or whatever patristic commentary of non-Alexandrian type you like: you will find them always explaining New Testament prophecies as coming to fulfilment in the interpreter's own time. What was said about "battles and wars, famines and pestilences, and earthquakes" was always easy to be identified with some events of the time. There were always some heretics able to be stamped as the Antichrist or his prophet. Wyclifites,

Hussites, the Reformers recognised the Antichrist sitting in the temple of God in the Pope, whilst, on the other hand, the Jesuits easily found marks of the Antichrist in Luther or Calvin. Later on there was Napoleon as the beast from the abyss, or the railway as the dragon with his tail—in our time it would be the motor-cars. At all events it was always something of the interpreter's own time. You had only to open your eyes and to look around you to see that the time was fulfilled and the end at hand.

This form of interpretation, which we may call the historical adaptation of eschatological prophecy, was the most widely spread. Former times had only two alternatives besides, viz., the spiritualising interpretation of the Alexandrian school, which rather tended to abolish all eschatological ideas, and another one, which one may speak of as a really eschatological interpretation; there were only a few exceptional men who, disregarding the usual view, maintained that the predictions of those marvellous supernatural events which are spoken of in the New Testament were to be taken in a very strict sense, so that it would be impossible to identify them with anything in the ordinary course of history. You have, they declared, to expect them as they are foretold, but we do not know at what time they will happen; it may be in some few years, it may be in some hundred years, because, as has been said already in the second Epistle of St. Peter, "*A thousand years are with the Lord as one day.*"

It is very interesting to see on this point St. Augustine's correspondence with the Bishop of Salona, Hesychius.[1] To speak

[1] Epp. 197, 198, 199 in Migne, PL 33, 899–925.

in general terms, this view, supported first by Irenaeus, found a stronger support only in more recent times. It was the so-called first Tübingen school—not that critical one of F. Chr. Baur, but an earlier one, founded by Storr and represented in Baur's own time by J. T. Beck. Quite evangelical in type, these theologians put themselves against all spiritualising as much as Bishop Nepos or Methodius in the third century had contradicted the spiritualising interpretation of Origen. We may remark that there had been always a realistic tradition in western interpretation. So Bengel and the Tübingen men laid much stress on the realistic meaning of New Testament eschatology, but they neglected altogether that element of nearness in the prophecies which, taken strictly, would never allow a hundred or thousand years to be put between prediction and fulfilment.

2. With the eighteenth century interpretation became historical, and thus only the question arose: what was the meaning of the men who uttered those predictions? Certainly they did not think about events of the second or fourth, or even the nineteenth century. By saying "*what will shortly come to pass*" they did not mean to say "*shortly*" for Hippolytus or for Cyril, nor even for Swedenborg, but "*shortly*" for themselves. They must have been thinking of the last things as being at hand. But how did they conceive them? Was it really to be understood verbally, exactly as the words used suggest, something almost supernatural, but at the same time visible, and to be touched, —some divine miraculous change of the whole external order of things,—or was it rather to be understood in a spiritual sense of something moral and inward?

There were at first only very few voices who supported the former view, which hardly could be brought into line with modern ideas. The majority of interpreters tried to escape from the difficulty by returning to the allegorising method of Origen. We quite understand that the average of modern theology, influenced as it was by Greek philosophy on one side, and by the predominant ethical ideas of the gospel on the other, could not do otherwise than spiritualise what was said by Christ and His apostles. It was in particular Schleiermacher's school, but also the critical school of Baur, which renewed the old spiritualising allegory. The whole school of Vermittelungs-theologen, as we usually call them, as well as the liberals of former times, acknowledged nothing but religious and moral ideas in the teaching of Jesus. The eschatological utterances, interpreted in this way, lost all their significance and became rather a duplicate of other sayings put into an awkward picturesque form: so—it was argued—we had better neglect them and keep to the clearer utterances of the Fourth Gospel. You may take the Biblical theology of the late Professor Willibald Beyschlag, of Halle, as the average expression of this standpoint in Germany. We find it supported even at the present day by, for instance, the late Professor Erich Haupt, of Halle,[1] and by Professor Adams Brown, of New York.[2]

But this spiritualising interpretation does too much violence to the actual words of the Gospel. It could not stand the attack

[1] *Die eschatologischen Aussagen Jesu in den synoptischen Evangelien*, 1895.

[2] Art. *Parousia* in Hastings DB, iii. 674–680, 1900.

of a more realistic feeling in New Testament theology. Professor B. Weiss, of Berlin, simply by collecting all that is to be found in the Gospels, demonstrated clearly that there are many really eschatological ideas. I should mention here a very important English contribution, published for the first time without the author's name in 1878 with the title, *The Parousia, a critical inquiry into the New Testament Doctrine of our Lord's Second Coming;* in a new edition of 1887 the author's name was added—J. S. Russell. I do not know who he was, but at all events he was a very sincere Bible-reader. He made it quite clear that you cannot deal with the New Testament prophecies in the way of former interpreters, taking them as referring to a much later time, nor put them aside by reading something spiritual into them; you have to take them as they are: foretelling some great catastrophe in the lifetime of Jesus' own generation. When he comes to the end of his investigation, he puts the difficulty in the form of the following dilemma: either you have to say with some rationalists, Jesus and His apostles were wrong in their expectation; or if you believe in the divine truth of the Bible, you must explain it by some event of the apostolic time, and you will easily find this in the destruction of Jerusalem.

Now, as a matter of fact, this solution of the question is a very old one. It has its Biblical support in the writings of St. Luke, who, as we shall see in our next lecture, colours the eschatological utterances in such a way that they may be understood of the destruction of Jerusalem. It has always had some support by later interpretation.[1] But it will not prove

[1] This historical orientation of Jesus' predic-

itself to be the final solution of the problem.

3. By modern research we have become acquainted with much apocalyptic literature, produced by later Judaism and highly appreciated in the early Christian Church, but forgotten for many centuries. We owe their discovery and collection to such scholars as Dillmann, Volkmar, Hilgenfeld, Schürer, and to English scholars, in the first rank of whom I should mention Professor R. H. Charles, besides Dr. Taylor, the late Master of St. John's, Cambridge,

tions is the main feature in the most recent contribution to our subject by H. B. Sharman, *The Teaching of Jesus about the future according to the Synoptic Gospels*, Chicago, 1909. Cp. also Canon Grierson's pamphlet on *Christ's Predictions of His Return* in *The Churchman*, Dec., 1908, who maintains that Christ was conscious of His cosmic relations and foreknew His manifold comings in the epoch-making crisis of history.

Rendel Harris and F. C. Conybeare. By reading this apocalyptic literature we became aware of a very important feature, not noted before, viz., that the eschatological ideas, or, as I would rather say, the forms in which they were uttered, were by no means an original product of the Gospel, but are taken over from later Judaism. This means that we have to explain them by an eschatological tradition. There was a certain amount of eschatological views spread in Judaism, being a part of what we call the "Weltanschauung," the general view of the world, prevailing at that time. And even Jesus and His disciples were participators of it; their horizon was not wider in this respect than that of their countrymen.

So a quite new form of interpretation appeared, the utterances of the Gospels being explained by Jewish eschatology. It was Joh. Weiss, in his book, *Die Predigt Jesu vom Reiche Gottes*, 1892, second edition, 1900, who started this new form with a rare success.[1] The current notions of the gospel were all to be taken in the realistic sense of late Judaism; the eschatological prophecies of Jesus were to be understood from his Jewish conceptions, without any regard to their fulfilment. There is a strong tendency now among German interpreters to get rid of their own modern views with the aim of looking at the early Christian writings with early Christian eyes, a tendency which you would call perhaps Romanticism, but is, however, better styled historical sincerity com-

[1] The influence of J. Weiss may best be seen in the second edition of H. Wendt, *Die Lehre Jesu*, 1901, where we have the most deliberate and circumspect judgment pronounced upon this eschatological view.

bined with some antiquarian feeling. They enlarge intentionally the difference between early and recent Christian views as much as possible with the purpose of being historical as far as possible.[1] The best example of this one-sided archaism may be found in Kabisch's book on Pauline eschatology (1893). But there are many other contributions of the same style in Germany now. In this way we got used to these rather strange eschatological ideas, so that many of our recent German students will find themselves quite at home in them and will think this form of interpretation to be the usual, the only natural one.

4. This is not all. Quite recently the problem of eschatology has gained yet another aspect. We have learned not only

[1] Cp. the present writer's paper: *Der gegenwärtige Stand der Neutestamentlichen Exegese*, 1906.

to deal with the notions of Jesus and His disciples, and to explain them by contemporary views, but to ask for the practical significance of these views for those who held them. It is one of the great merits of Professor H. J. Holtzmann, formerly of Strassburg,[1] that he showed how to combine both these modes of dealing with the question, not only to collect and explain the single utterances, but to make out their importance as influencing Jesus' whole life. There has been always some tendency in this direction in Strassburg theology. It was Tim. Colani[2] who first

[1] Besides his *Lehrbuch der Neutestamentlichen Theologie*, 1897, I would recommend in connexion with our question especially his masterful little treatise, *Das Messianische Bewusstsein Jesu*, 1907, which gives an accurate summary of the present stand, together with a complete record of recent contributions.

[2] *Jésus Christ et les croyances messianiques de son temps*, 1869.

threw light upon the life of Jesus from the point of view of eschatology. From Strassburg started W. Baldensperger, now Professor at Giessen.[1] Professor F. Spitta, of Strassburg, has the great merit of always getting fresh lights upon the story of the Gospels out of those late Jewish apocryphas, going hand in hand with Joh. Weiss in their realistic interpretation. So you will easily understand how it came to pass that one of the most clever junior Strassburg men, Dr. Albert Schweitzer, also well known as an ingenious interpreter of Bach's music, happened to put forth his so-called theory of "consequent eschatology," *i.e.* that Jesus in all His acting is to be understood by nothing else than His eschatological view that He was

[1] *Das Selbstbewusstsein Jesu im Lichte der messianischen Hoffnungen seiner Zeit*, 1888; second edition 1892, third edition 1903 (part I.).

designed by the Father to bring an end unto all things. Now I wonder how it happened that this theory, put forth in the form of a history, or rather an historical review, of the research on the life of Christ in the last hundred years "from Reimarus to Wrede," 1906, met with much more appreciation in England than in Germany, where even Schweitzer's friends were rather surprised by the one-sidedness of his views and declined to follow him. I need refer only to the criticism made upon the book by Professor P. Wernle (Basle),[1] by Professor Ad. Jülicher (Marburg),[2] and last, not least, Professor H. J. Holtzmann[3]

[1] In *Theol. Literaturzeitung*, 1906, N. 18, Sp. 501 ff.

[2] In his lectures *Neue Linien in der Kritik der evangelischen Überlieferung*, 1906, 1–13.

[3] In his reviews *Der gegenwärtige Stand der Leben-Jesu-Forschung*, *Deutsche Literaturzeitung*, 1906, N. 38 ff.

—while Professor W. Sanday's treatment of the book in his work, *The Life of Christ in Recent Research*, 1907, gave Dr. Schweitzer's book a splendid advertisement in this country and, at the Oxford Congress for the history of religions in 1908, Professor F. C. Burkitt[1] made himself champion of this theory of consistent eschatology, which I myself would prefer to call radical eschatology.

Now, without going into the question itself, which will be our task in the next lectures, I may be allowed to say only this: if eschatology is the key to all gospel-

[1] See his paper on *The Parable of the Wicked Husbandmen*, Transactions, II. 321–328, and cp. also his essay *The Eschatological Idea in the Gospel* in Essays on some Biblical Questions of the day, by Members of the University of Cambridge, 1909, 193–213. Unnecessary to say, that Prof. Burkitt does not share all the conclusions of Dr. Schweitzer!

questions, then it becomes the problem of problems how Christianity could go on without eschatology through so many centuries. If there was nothing in Jesus but eschatology, then He was a misguided enthusiast, and it would be almost impossible to explain how the name of an eccentric became the symbol for millions and millions of Christians who took from Him not only some vain hopes of the future, but a joyful experience of real salvation and an unexampled amount of moral energy.

The exaggerated "Consistency," however, should not keep back others from following the method in a sounder way—this was rightly maintained by Professor K. Lake at the Congress.[1] We have a very

[1] See also the remarkable book of H. Monnier, *La mission historique de Jésus*, 1906; and Abbé

remarkable instance thereof in a recent American contribution by Professor Shailer Matthews: *The Messianic Hope in the New Testament*, 1905, a book whose very title, when compared with Dr. Kennedy's well-known book on *St. Paul's Conception of the Last Things*, 1904,[1] shows how much the view has changed: it is not the material of eschatological notions and doctrines, but it is their living force and influence upon the piety and the whole life of their believers, which is discussed here.

At this point we may stop our historical inquiry into the different ways of dealing with our problem.

Loisy's *Les évangiles synoptiques*, 1907–8, together with the fair criticism pronounced in C. Piepenoning, *Jésus historique*, 1909.

[1] Cp. also W. O. E. Oesterley, B.D., *The doctrine of the Last Things, Jewish and Christian*, 1908.

II

The word eschatology has very different meanings. There was a time, some fifty years ago, and it lasts perhaps till now, when people, talking about eschatology, did not mean to say anything else than what happens after death: "*It is appointed unto men once to die, and after this cometh judgment*" (Heb. ix. 27). Now we know better that eschatology is the doctrine of the last things as understood by late Jewish teaching. And latterly we have come to use the word now to express a certain mode of feeling, not so much the different opinions on some points of eschatology as the whole fashion of mind produced by the belief in a near approach of the end. It is in this last sense that the word is taken here, viz., as signifying some idea which exercised a spiritual influence on the mind of Jesus and His disciples.

To understand this we must bear in mind what the belief of Jewish people in regard to the last things was in former times, and what was the evolution which this belief underwent.

1. The religion of Israel was, as you know, national in a far stricter sense than we can use this word of the religions of the Greeks or the Romans or other peoples. It meant not only that every member of the nation by his birth was to be an adherent of this religion, but that the very subject of the religion was the nation, not the individual. Israel as a nation was the chosen people of God; it was in the nation's history that God revealed Himself to mankind, it was to the people that He had given all His promises, the individuals having no right

for themselves, but only as members of the nation. It was their happiness to belong to this chosen people of God, and their hope and aim that their children or grandchildren perhaps would participate in the glorious fulfilment of God's promises to His people. To be sure, at a later time, let us say from the time of the Maccabean revival, a more individualistic conception began to spread among the Jewish people: it may have been suggested by the individualistic doctrines of the Persian religion, as some recent scholars maintain, or it may have come out of this very Hellenistic influence, so strong at the time, against which the Maccabean movement was directed. Its deeper source, however, is to be looked for in the Maccabean movement itself: the Jews of this time, prepared as they were by Persian and Hellenistic conceptions, could not think of God as leaving without any personal reward those who gave up even their life for His sake. It appeared to them impossible, incompatible with God's righteousness, that the martyrs should die without any compensation. It was as a benefit on behalf of the martyrs that Jewish religion asked at first for a personal continuation of life after death. But note: it is not a continuation in our sense of the word. Death comes in and separates body and soul. Neither of them is living when separated from the other. They are both in an estate of unconscious existence which you may rightly compare to sleep. The body is in the tomb, the soul in the so-called Sheôl, which is not to be identified with Hell, but rather with the Hades of the Greeks, where the souls live their life as shades. This existence—

if we may call it existence, being quite unconscious—lasts until that great day when God fulfils His promises to the nation. Then, but only then, those who are to participate in this glorious and happy time of salvation will be awakened, both body and soul will come out of their different receptacles, and will be united, and so the man will be able to enjoy a new life in company with all those who are alive then. So, you see, the old national conception of the last things has not given place to another one of more Hellenistic and individualistic type; it is still the old Jewish notion of the nation as the subject, only enlarged by the idea of a bodily resurrection of some earlier members of the people.

There is a splendid sermon of the late Principal John Caird, of Glasgow, in his University sermons, upon Hebrews

xi. 39, 40: "And these all having obtained a good report through faith, received not the promise, God having provided some better thing for us that they without us should not be made perfect." Dealing with the idea of "Comparative resurrection" the Principal says some most beautiful and stimulating things of great practical value for the religious life. But he treats the question as a matter of speculation, and not having first gone through these late Jewish conceptions, he misses just the one important point to be noticed from the standpoint of the modern historical method, viz., that we have in those words the Christian adaptation of that Jewish notion: salvation will come for all those who deserve it, but only when it comes for the nation.

This view is quite different from what

we are accustomed to, and I would like the reader clearly to understand the great importance of this difference. The Jewish conception, by keeping to the national idea, has always an historical orientation: it is based upon that notion of two ages, one which is now, and another to come; the present bad, sinful, full of oppression, the future good, holy, happy. On the other hand, Greek, and later Christian thought, more individualising in its nature, goes rather in the line of a local than of a temporal contrast: happiness is not here, but you can find it elsewhere. Or, to make this a little more clear, one might say that, in the case of the Jews, possibility of salvation, being an expectation and not yet a reality, caused the stress to be laid upon the time *when*, while in the case of the Greeks, possibility of salvation being conceived as a present fact, caused the stress to be laid upon the place *where*.[1] You know the islands of the Hesperides far in the West, where the happy heroes enjoyed a god-like, everlasting life; you know the two parts in the Hades, one dark and harmful, a real hell for the sinners, the other a bright and happy abode for pious and righteous men. In the latest stage of Greek religion and philosophy it is rather the contrast of above and below, of heaven and earth. And you see that this is what most Christian people think of as the original Christian conception: that after their life on this sorrowful earth has come to an end, they immediately will go to another life, a life of glory and happiness in

[1] Or better still, as my friend Professor Lake put it in a conversation, we had, after attending this lecture, "the Jew is separated from the realm of bliss by time, the Greek by space."

heaven. This is what they call salvation. Now without entering into the dogmatic question of what will happen to us after death, we may safely say that this is not the original Christian conception of salvation, which was almost in the line of Jewish thought, not perhaps so much national, but collective, historical: a time was to be expected when all who believed and placed their hope in God as the Saviour of His faithful people should see His glorious salvation, not only the quick, but also those who had died before, because they would rise again at that very moment.

2. This salvation might be conceived in many different ways: the mass of Jewish people took it in a political sense, either purely national: viz., that the yoke of heathen tyranny should be broken off, and Israel, free from all oppression, should

enjoy his own land, his Holy City with the temple of God, and live a happy life under his God's gracious guidance, God's royalty being identified with the dominion of Israel over all other nations. Or else the conception was rather mixed up with party-morals: the salvation would come for that very part of Israel which remained faithful to the Lord their God, which, humble and poor, had to stand the oppression by that proud, rich company of unrighteous and godless men, who ruled, by their own will, over God's people, so that the salvation was to be seen in a true restoration of the theocracy against the tyranny of the Hasmonean or Sadducean priests or princes like Herod and his sons. Besides these there was a third form of conception, which, compared with the two political ones already mentioned, may be called mythological, as it deals not so much with human powers in opposition to God's kingdom, but with the spiritual powers of the devil and his demons, always in rebellion against God, and trying to make men offend against God's holy will and law with the aim of bringing them under their own pitiless dominion.

There are only a few traces of this last conception in pre-Christian Jewish eschatology, especially in the book of Enoch, where the fallen angels, the so-called Egregores (watchmen), play a great part.

Now we may say that in whatever way salvation was conceived, the very aim of Jewish religion was to get this salvation, not so much to ensure a share in it (because most Jews supposed this to be their natural right), but to get God to bring it. Because it was not to be brought by means of human operation. It was supposed to be a quite superhuman, supernatural acting by God Himself, sending His salvation to His people. Only that this faithful people may influence His motion by pressing on Him in prayer, fasting and doing His ordinances in the law. As to how God would do it, there was no certainty; either He would come by Himself, breaking open the heaven and descending, or He would send His Messiah, the blessed one, His beloved, His Son, the Son of man, the Son of David. This coming would be preceded by various signs. The heathen power would rise to an almost unheard of level of tyranny, cruelty and abomination, the iniquity of the godless and unrighteous would join with them, so that the apostasy from the one God, the living and true one, and His worship to the idols and all the sins of idolatry would become general; there would be signs in the heaven and on earth, the sun giving no more light, the moon being changed into blood, the stars falling from heaven, earthquakes, famines, pestilences, frightening mankind everywhere. Then at the very culmination of horrors the Messiah would appear in a miraculous way, and by His wonderful power He would destroy all His enemies, and by the aid of His angels collect His chosen people from all parts of the world, and reign over them in justice and peace, filled as He was with God's Holy Spirit, the Spirit of righteousness and truth.

3. It is not necessary to go further into detail now, because all this is very well known, especially through the works of Professor Charles. We only repeat, that there was no self-consistent doctrine of eschatology among the Jews of Jesus' time, and that the influence of eschatology was rather restricted to some circles, the life

of the people being occupied by the business of the present time and ruled by the heavy yoke of Pharisaic ordinances. It was really something new to the people when John the Baptist started his preaching in the wilderness of Judæa: "*Repent ye, for the kingdom of heaven is at hand.*"

And whatever may have been the position taken by Jesus in regard to eschatology, there can be no doubt that eschatology was much more important in early Christianity than in late Judaism. It was so, because the messianic hope had found in Jesus its proper object: since Jesus had appeared, people were convinced that His glorious advent (the Parousia) was to be expected at the earliest term. This is the main distinction between early Christian and late Jewish eschatology: all has received a stricter form, many possibilities being excluded by the very fact that it was Jesus, with all His personal characteristics, who was to be expected; all has been brought nearer, the fact that the Messiah was known, that it was Jesus, and that Jesus had disappeared only for a short time, giving urgency to all expectations. There was even an increasing tendency towards eschatological occupation in the second half of the first century, the very time when our Gospels were written. So the problem comes before us, whether the eschatology of the Gospels belongs to the original stock of Jesus-tradition, or is due to this later eschatological inclination of Christianity, which, borrowing from Judaism, transformed the gospel into a rather eschatological teaching. It is lastly the question, how far Jesus can be brought under the law of historical continuity, He Himself being dependent backwards on late Judaism and influencing forwards early Christianity

—and how far He must be regarded as an exceptional being outside the operation of this law, unrooted in His nation, and misunderstood by His followers.

Various Tendencies in the Transmission of the Gospel. The Eschatological Stock of Jesus-Tradition

LECTURE II

VARIOUS TENDENCIES IN THE TRANSMISSION OF THE GOSPEL. THE ESCHATOLOGICAL STOCK OF JESUS-TRADITION

HAVING defined the problem as it stands to-day in our first lecture, we now go on to try to settle first what is the Gospel-tradition about eschatology, and what measure of certainty we have to make out our Lord's own words and meaning.

I

There is not only some vague possibility of alterations brought into the Gospel in the course of its transmission, but there is plenty of evidence that sayings of Jesus were coloured afterwards, and this at first [*A*] by eschatological additions and changes. We may confine our investigation to three instances:

1. The saying against those who say "Lord, Lord" is given by Matthew vii. 21 and Luke vi. 46, both passages belonging to the sermon on the mount. In Matthew vii. 22, 23 herewith is combined another saying, which is found in Luke xiii. 25–27 in quite a different context. We are not concerned here with this second saying—we may remark by the way that Luke has evidently the original form, not only in the shape of the parable, but also in the features claimed by the unfortunate people outdoors, which are with Luke rather ordinary experiences of Jesus' lifetime while Matthew puts in extraordinary

experiences of the apostolic age;—at all events, this second word is eschatological in its substance: it deals with the last judgment. Not so the first saying; as it runs in Luke, "*And why call ye me, Lord, Lord, and do not the things which I say?*" there is nothing in it, which tends towards eschatology. Now there can be hardly any doubt that Luke has the original form of this saying, and that the Matthæan form "*Not every one that says unto me Lord, Lord,* SHALL ENTER INTO THE KINGDOM OF HEAVEN, *but he that doeth the will of my Father which is in heaven,*" with its unmistakable eschatological colouring, strengthened by the introduction of "*in that day*" in the next sentence, is due to the combination with that other saying. It is a well-known feature in the composition of our First Gospel—and we shall see other instances of the same immediately—that words are brought into a closer connexion by conforming them one to the other.

The priority of the non-eschatological form of this saying is supported (1) by the parable which follows immediately in Luke and only a few verses later on in Matthew as well in quite the same form, so that we may trace it back to Q, the parable, I mean, of the house built on the rock or upon the sand, a parable which is not likely to be taken in an eschatological sense; and (2) by the comparison of another saying which has much affinity to it, Jesus' saying about His relations: "*For whosoever shall do the will of God, the same is my brother, and sister, and mother*" (Mark iii. 35; cp. Matt. xii. 50, Luke viii. 21). It is not said: I will, at the day of judgment, declare him to be my brother, &c., but "*he is.*" So it is a purely moral statement without the peculiar taste of eschatology. And this is all the more remarkable as it is found in the Marcan tradition.

2. The next instance of this kind of transformation I find in the parables of the tares and of the net, forming originally a couple of parables as so many others, now separated in Matthew xiii. 24–30 (with an additional interpretation in v. 36–43) and xiii. 47–50. The evangelist sees in both parables a description of the last judgment, when "*the Son of Man shall send forth his angels and they shall gather out of his kingdom all things that cause stumbling, and them that do iniquity, and shall cast them into the furnace of fire, there shall be the weeping and gnashing of teeth. Then shall the righteous shine forth as the sun in the kingdom of their Father.*" "*The harvest is the end of the world,*" xiii. 39, this is the main point of

Matthew's interpretation, from which all the parable is to be explained. But take the parables by themselves, and you will see that there is no necessity for this interpretation. Jesus is not describing a single act but something which occurs to men at any time. As sowing and harvest are repeated annually and the gathering and sifting of fishes is the fisherman's daily work, so it is some rule for daily life which Jesus put into the disciples' mind by telling them these parables. Many interpreters since the time of Tertullian have found here some rule of ecclesiastical conduct: the Church as a *corpus mixtum* has to contain sinners as well as saints until the day of God's judgment. But this is neither the meaning of the evangelist, who in his allegorical interpretation makes the field signify the world, not the Church, and neglects the servants of the householder altogether, the problem Matthew is interested in being not the composition of the Christian Church and the conduct of its leaders on account of bad members, but the situation of Christianity in the midst of the world of unbelievers, a close parallel to John xvii. 11, 14: "*These are in the world,*" "*not of the world.*" Nor is it the original meaning of the parable, this giving merely the general moral rule: "Do not put in your hands before things are ready; everything will, at the proper time, be revealed for what it is; leave it to God's care—the same rule as we have it in the famous counsel of Gamaliel, Acts v. 35 ff.

3. The main instance of this intrusion of eschatology into the Gospel-tradition is the great eschatological sermon found in Mark xiii., Matthew xxiv. and Luke xxi. It was in the year 1864 that Colani and Weizsäcker, one independent of the other,

came to the conclusion that this is not the report of an original sermon of Jesus, but a composite work, mixing original sayings of Christ with parts of a little apocalypse, as to the origin of which there was and is still some difference of opinion, some scholars maintaining with Weizsäcker, that it was a Jewish document, while the majority agrees in acknowledging the Christian character and is inclined to identify this little apocalyptic fly-leaf with the revelation spoken of by Eusebius, *H.E.* III. v. 3, as having caused the Christians to move from the Holy City before its fall. As reconstructions of this little apocalypse are easily accessible, *e.g.*, in Professor Charles' book on Eschatology, I may confine myself to a few remarks: (1) As we have only Mark (Matthew borrowing from Mark[1] and Luke colour-

[1] I do not think that two or three instances,

ing Mark's narrative), it is impossible to reconstruct the actual words of Mark's source; it contained probably verses 7, 8, 14–20, 24–27; but it is uncertain if some words, such as verses 15 and 18, are perhaps additions by Mark, and, on the other hand, if we have to add verses 21–23 and perhaps also verse 30. (2) We find described only a few remarkable features: in the first part, the beginnings of horrors, a general motion and revolution among the peoples and all kinds of frightful events; in the second part, the culmination of horrors, something mysterious, Mark using the same words as Daniel, but contrary to the Greek gender as a masculine, showing thereby that he thinks of an individual, some Antichrist. With

given by B. Weiss and others, are enough to prove that Matthew had independent knowledge of that apocalypse.

the notion of supreme horror are com bined two different ideas of getting out of them: a *local* one—flying into the mountains, and this is the pet point of the little apocalypse, marked by calling the attention of the reader (you see it is not a sermon of Jesus); and on the other hand a *temporal* one—shortening of the time by the powerful interfering of the Lord (you see again, it is not Jesus who is speaking here); and in the third part, through a terrible motion of all the elements, the glorious advent of the Messiah. There is in all this, not even in the last part, nothing of peculiar Christian notions which we ought to trace back to Jesus Himself. They are common apocalyptic ideas. And yet, all is so short, so brief in this little apocalypse, nothing unnecessary, only main points. This is, I believe, the proof-mark of early Christian in comparison with late

Jewish literature, according to Wellhausen's well-known remark regarding the Gospel and rabbinic literature: that all that is in the Gospel is to be found there too, yes, all, and much more. It is especially the lack of all national and political elements in this much-condensed little apocalypse which makes it quite clear—as far as I may be able to pronounce judgment—that the conception is an early Christian one, using the materials of late Jewish eschatology in its own way. (3) The very fact that Mark could give this little apocalypse as a sermon of Jesus, taken together with this other fact, that several words of the apocalypse have parallels in well-attested sayings of Jesus[1] and that the sayings

[1] Cp. Mark xiii. 15, 16 with Luke xvii. 31; Mark xiii. 21–23 with Luke xvii. 23; Matt. xxiv. 26; especially Mark xiii. 26 with viii. 38 and xiv. 62.

combined with the apocalypse in Mark xiii. bear nearly the same stamp,[1] proves that the main ideas of this little fly-leaf are not far removed from Jesus' own opinions. But the fact remains, that it is an eschatological addition to the original Jesus-tradition.[2]

These three instances of alteration by intrusion of eschatology could easily be multiplied. But if one were to conclude that all eschatological material found actually in the Gospel was but later addition

[1] So Mark xiii. 6 is nearly identical with xiii. 21 f.=Luke xvii. 23.

[2] Mark, taking this little apocalypse from about 68 A.D. into his gospel, has his analogon in the author of Q, putting into Jesus' mouth a quotation from an apocryphal book of Wisdom dating probably not earlier than 69 A.D. [the Zacharias son of Barachia being identical with the one mentioned by Josephus, B. J. IV. v. 4 (335)], *see* Luke xi. 49–51, Matt. xxiii. 34–36.

or transformation, one would be wide of the mark. False generalisation is the worst of all faults in method. Plenty of eschatological sayings remain, which must come from original tradition.

Before starting, however, our proper investigation, let us turn to another form of alteration [*B*], eschatological utterances of Jesus being transfigured into historical predictions—especially by Luke.

1. There is, *e.g.*, Christ's saying in regard to Jerusalem, taken evidently from Q, both in Matthew xxiii. 37–39 and Luke xiii. 34–35. The closing words: "*And I say unto you, Ye shall not see me, until ye shall say, Blessed is he that cometh in the name of the Lord,*" are capable of a twofold interpretation, either eschatological or—as they recur at Jesus' entrance into Jerusalem—historical. Now Luke placing the saying long before this

entrance, understood probably, and liked his readers to understand, in the latter sense: an historical prediction of the Messianic entrance: whereas Matthew, recording the word only after this entrance, took it evidently in an eschatological sense. And he was right in his understanding, as far as I can see.

2. A similar instance of transformation is given in Luke's reproduction of Mark xiii., the already mentioned synoptic apocalypse: "*The abomination of desolation,*" spoken of by Mark and Matthew as *standing where* HE *ought not* (or *in the holy place*, Matthew) is paraphrased by Luke xxi. 20 in the following way: "*But when ye see Jerusalem compassed with armies, then know that her* DESOLATION *is at hand.*" It is the same word ἐρήμωσις, used here instead of some more usual expressions for destruction, as καταστροφή, καθαίρεσις, καταβολή, ἀνατροπή, which

betrays Luke borrowing from the Danielic formula in Mark and taking the mysterious expression in the sense of some prophetic utterances.[1] In this way he substitutes definite historical prediction for an obscure eschatological prophecy.[2]

[1] ἐρήμωσις is found in LXX=חָרְבָּה in Jer. vii. 34, xxii. 5, xxxii. 18, li. 6, 22, but connected with γῆ, in connexion with Jerusalem in Daniel ix. 2. Josephus uses ἅλωσις *B. J.* I. i. 4 (10); VI. x. 1 (441), sometimes κατασκαφή, ibid. VI. x. 1 (440). For other equivalents see *Corpus glossariorum latinorum* ed. Loewe et Goetz, vi. 333, s.v. *destructio.*

[2] Another view has been proposed recently by my friend, Professor F. Spitta, in a suggestive study, "Die grosse eschatologische Rede Jesu" in *Theol. Stud. u. Krit.*, 1909, 348–401; retracting his own former hypothesis of a Jewish apocalypse inserted in Matt. xxiv., Spitta maintains that Luke gives the original form of Jesus' answer to His disciples, the genuine prediction of the destruction of the temple being changed

If this be granted we have to reckon with the possibility that the number of eschatological sayings found in the earliest tradition has undergone diminution as well as enrichment by later alterations.

II.

We now proceed to ask how much there is of assured eschatological matter in the sayings of our Lord.

1. To begin with the main object of His preaching; the kingdom of God is in its origin undoubtedly an entirely eschatological notion. It is not God's government over the world, not His ruling His people, as usually in the Psalter, when there is said, "God rules," "God is king," but it is a peculiar

in Caligula's time into the apocalyptic notion known from Daniel.

estate of things when God is reigning without any opposition, neither by man, nor by the evil spirits. Now as John the Baptist (Matt. iii. 2) preaches that this kingdom of God is at hand,[1] so the preaching of Jesus begins with the very same announcement: "*the time is fulfilled and the kingdom of God is at hand*" (Mark i. 15; cp. Matt iv. 17). We have perhaps a still better instance of this in the Lord's prayer: if Jesus makes His disciples pray: "*Thy kingdom come,*" then it is not to be taken as already come but as to be hoped and

[1] We may perhaps be not allowed to take these words as a genuine rendering of John's message, because in Mark i. 4, 8 and Luke iii. 3, 7 ff. as well as in Matt. iii. 7 ff. he is represented rather as announcing an almost severe judgment. But this has to be taken only as a beginning or rather the means of making way for the kingdom of God.

prayed for. The next petition, given only by Matthew, "*Thy will be done, as in heaven, so on earth,*" makes it clear what the kingdom of God was understood to be: a moral estate of mankind wherein God's will was done without exception, without any opposition by personal sin or by contrary forces in society. The kingdom of God, as it would be conceived by those people who heard Jesus preaching, was to be something most desirable, an estate of complete happiness, something that was worthy the hardest efforts and even the greatest loss; you ought to give everything for it, even your own life. But at the same time people would understand that it was something to be looked for which you cannot make by your own efforts, but you have to wait for it until God brings it about.

2. Now the main question is for us as it was for the men of that time: What was the relation of Jesus to this kingdom of God? Except two or three passages which we are to consider later on, He never says that He is bringing it into being, but He speaks of Himself as of the Son of Man, a title which, as we know already, had a Messianic content; He never says directly that He is the Messiah; He even declines to be called the Son of David. And yet His whole appearance, the way He manifests Himself and the authoritative tone which He adopts show that He is the very kind of man to proclaim Himself the Messiah. And at last, when He is set before the High Court of the people and asked in the most solemn way by the High Priest upon His claim: "*Art thou the Christ, the Son of the Blessed?*" then

He said: "*I am, and ye shall see the Son of Man sitting at the right hand of power, and coming with the clouds of heaven* (Mark xiv. 61, 62). This is an unmistakable expression of His claim for Messiahship. And even if we would prefer the form in which Matthew xxvi. 64 puts the words: "*Thou hast said; nevertheless I say unto you, henceforth ye shall see the Son of Man sitting at the right hand of power, and coming on the clouds of heaven*," we ought to say that it is a form of restrained assertion which we may paraphrase: Yes, but it is not I who have used the actual word, but thou hast used it.

Now it seems to me to be impossible to maintain, as some scholars do, that Jesus denies his Messiahship altogether (so Dalman, Merx), or that He makes a distinction between Himself and the

Messiah to be expected according to the words of Psalm cx. 1 and Daniel vii. 13. With more probability it has been said that He claims Messiahship not as His present state, but only for a future time. He is not the Messiah, but He will be the Messiah. This notion of a Messiah to come, first put forth, so far as I know, by Joh. Weiss, has met with an almost unusual degree of assent. It has been accepted by H. Holtzmann, A. Harnack,[1] H. Monnier,[2] A. Loisy, and many others. Indeed, there are some difficulties in the life of Jesus which would find the easiest explanation by assuming that Jesus, persuaded as He was that He was the Son of

[1] *Sprüche und Reden Jesu* (= Beiträge II.), 1907, 169.

[2] *La mission historique de Jésus*, 1906, 64.

God, the chosen one to bring salvation, nevertheless, conceived Himself not to be the Messiah, but only to be destined to be the Messiah in a later time: *Messias destinatus, Messias futurus.* His appearance, resembling rather a rabbi or at most a prophet, was so far from the popular notion of the Messiah, who should be a glorious and mighty king, destroying all his enemies by means of his power, that we easily could imagine Him taking His present appearance only as a preparatory one, His office being to prepare the people for His coming in glory as the Messiah. So He would have been His own forerunner, His own John the Baptist. But this was not His view, neither was it the opinion of His judges. The question laid before Him by the High Priest was, "*Art thou the Christ the Son of the Blessed?*" And

Jesus answered, "*I am.*" He did not tell them: "Not yet, but if you will bring Me to death, then I shall be it." He simply replied, "*I am, and you will see.*" The condemnation by the High Council as well as the accusation brought before the Roman Governor gives, I think, sufficient evidence that His claim on Messiahship was understood not as that of a Messiah destinatus, but as that of a present Messiah. It is just the contrast between this claim and the very appearance of this humble prisoner brought before him which puzzles Pilate so that he would have refused to execute the sentence, except for fear of the Jews, who frightened him by the Emperor's wrath. The title on the Cross is by itself a convincing argument against this modern theory of a Messiahship of the future.

3. It is quite certain, I should think, that Jesus claimed to be the Messiah. But it is equally certain that He speaks of His coming again in glory and power. If one would reject the testimony of Mark xiv. 62 pleading that there was none of the disciples present at the trial, one must accept the combined testimony of other utterances. When speaking about the necessity of confession he says: "*For whosoever shall be ashamed of me and of my words in this adulterous and sinful generation, the Son of Man also shall be ashamed of him, when he cometh in the glory of his Father with the holy angels*" (Mark viii. 38; cp. Matt. xvi. 27; Luke ix. 26). When asked by James and John to give them the places of honour on His right and on His left *in His glory*, as Mark x. 37, or *in His kingdom*, as Matthew xx. 21 puts the question, He

does not reject this notion, but only makes a very hard condition, and refers the right of bestowing those places to the Father (Mark x. 35–40; Matt. xx. 20–23).[1]

The warnings against false Messiahs (cp. Mark xiii. 6, 21, and Luke xvii. 23, 24, Matt. xxiv. 23–28) presuppose the idea of His own coming again.

There are many parables, dealing with the unexpected returning of the Lord, or the sudden coming of some one: Mark xiii. 33–37 gives only short extracts, which, however, show he knew a much larger tradition, which one may try to reconstruct

[1] This has a remarkable parallel in the promise given to the twelve that they shall take part in the messianic judgment sitting on twelve thrones (Matt. xix. 28; Luke xxii. 29, 30 [Q?]).

by the help of the First and Third Gospels.

So far we have gathered mainly from the Marcan tradition. Mark, it has been said, is the strongest supporter of eschatological views; and, in fact, there are some passages where the other main sources have a less eschatological colouring: not only Luke, who reproduces Jesus' answer to the High Priest without the closing sentence (*coming*, &c.), allowing, thereby, for a more spiritual interpretation of the rest (*sitting at the right hand*), and so weakening the eschatological impression, but also Q, of equal value with Mark in regard to the certainty of tradition; so instead of the words quoted above from Mark viii. 38, "*The Son of Man also shall be ashamed of him, when he cometh in the glory of his Father with the holy angels,*" we read in Q (Luke xii. 9 and Matt. x.

33) "*He that denieth me in the presence of men shall be denied in the presence of the angels of God*" (or according to Matthew, "*before my Father which is in heaven*"), a phrase which, intended to be understood in an eschatological sense, is capable, however, of a more spiritual interpretation not showing that peculiar note of time characteristic of Jewish eschatology.

But we must not generalise this fact and draw the conclusion that eschatology supported only or mostly by Mark is his own addition, and therefore not to be taken as a genuine part of Jesus' teaching. Neither Q nor the other non-Marcan sources of our Gospel-tradition are bare of eschatology; on the contrary, they support it strongly.

We have mentioned already the promise made to the disciples (Matt. xix. 28;

Luke xxii. 29–30); Jesus' woe over Jerusalem (Matt. xxiii. 39; Luke xiii. 35), with its final sentences: "*Ye shall not see me henceforth, till ye shall say: Blessed is He that cometh in the name of the Lord.*"

The admonition for readiness gains strength from the argument: "*For in an hour that ye think not the Son of Man cometh*" (Matt. xxiv. 44; cp. Luke xii. 40).

The coming of the Son of Man is said to be like a lightning (Matt. xxiv. 27; cp. Luke xvii. 24).

The want of vigilance and the carelessness of mankind before the coming of the Son of Man is compared with the state of mind in the days of Noah (Matt. xxiv. 37; cp. Luke xvii. 26).

All this shows that the notion of the coming of the Son of Man as something still to be expected is a commonplace in Gospel-tradition and has to be traced back to Jesus Himself.

4. There is another remark to be made in connexion with these utterances. It is hardly said anywhere how the coming of the Son of Man will be, except that it will be suddenly, surprising. Sometimes we find used the words of Daniel: "*on*" or "*with the clouds of heaven.*" Sometimes *angels* are spoken of as following Him. His *glory* is mentioned. If the single phrase is capable of a spiritualising interpretation, the impression made by the whole set of passages will be that it is some miraculous, supernatural, but at the same time external and visible event in history, or better still, some catastrophe at the very end of history; in one word, some really eschatological fact, which is meant.

It is important to settle this before we go on, because the spiritualising tendency of modern theology has tried to escape from this conclusion by dealing with every passage by itself. So making one after the other say what they were wanted to say, the interpreter was able to declare, that there is no eschatology at all.

Take, *e.g.*, Jesus' answer before the High Priest: "*Ye shall see the Son of Man sitting at the right hand of power, and coming with the clouds of heaven.*" Professor Haupt says: How can they see Him sitting at the right hand of power? this can be meant only in a spiritual way: they shall see His influence in the wonderful propagation of His gospel; and so the next sentence, and coming, &c., is but another illustration of the same idea: they will see His influence in the judgment passed upon their own people for having rejected Him. This seems quite probable But taken together with all the other utterances we have just considered, this explanation will hardly satisfy any one. If these words are spoken by Jesus—and I see no reason for denying this—they must be taken as they stand, as an expression for some really eschatological event.

5. A further point of no less importance is the following: Jesus says: "*Ye shall see.*" In connexion with a spiritual interpretation this may well be explained as comprehending not so much the judges themselves as their children and grandchildren and all other generations to follow. Taken together with our realistic interpretation it can only mean: you by yourselves, not men of a later time. The present generation is the latest. It is destined to live to see the end of all history.

This interpretation is confirmed by a set of sayings dealing with the notion of the present generation: We read in Mark xiii. 30, and in the parallel passages Matthew xxiv. 34, Luke xxi. 32, "*Verily I say unto you: This generation shall not pass away, until all these things be accomplished.*" As this saying is found in the eschatological chapter some writers maintain that it is a part of that fly-leaf which we found to be a later Christian apocalypse. This is possible, but I think it is equally possible and even more probable that it belongs to the genuine stock of sayings of Jesus, which were mixed up with that little apocalypse. At any rate, it is quite in the same line with those other words of Jesus, "*Ye shall see,*" &c.

It seems to be contradicted, however, by another saying. When asked by the Pharisees to give a sign from heaven,

Jesus sighed deeply in His spirit and said, "*Why doth this generation seek a sign? Verily, I say unto you: There shall no sign be given unto this generation.*" So Mark viii. 12. We are accustomed to another form of this answer, adding "*but the sign of Jonah.*" So we read in Matthew xvi. 4, the parallel passage to Mark viii. 12, as well as in Matthew xii. 39 and Luke xi. 29, two parallel passages taken probably from Q. Now as Matthew usually conforms the sayings he borrows from different sources, the testimony of Matthew xvi. 4 is of no value. We have in reality only Mark against Q, Q giving the additional words, Mark omitting them. Which form is genuine? Against the vast majority of writers I think Wellhausen is right here in maintaining the superiority of the Marcan tradition. Nobody until this day has succeeded in giving a fair explanation of what the sign of Jonah might mean. It is, I dare say, commonly acknowledged to-day that the interpretation given already by Matthew xii. 40 as pointing to the three days and three nights which Jonah spent in the whale's belly and Jesus likewise in the tomb or in Hell, is wrong. The preaching of Jonah, which caused the people of Nineveh to repent, can hardly be called a sign. Now, as our saying is combined in Q with another saying dealing with the repentance of the people of Nineveh at the preaching of Jonah, it seems to me highly probable that this other saying gave rise to the addition in the former saying, and that therefore Mark has preserved its original form. Jesus does not promise any sign, but He denies to the present generation the sign which they ask for, viz., the Messianic sign, which is, of course, to be distinguished from His powerful acts of mercy, these in the oldest tradition never being called σημεῖον sign. So Jesus by this answer denies that this generation will see the coming of the Messiah.

The contradiction between this saying and the other two sayings mentioned before, exists, I think, only in appearance. The solution is to be found in another saying, recorded by Mark ix. 1 (cp. Matt. xvi. 28 and Luke ix. 27): "*Verily I say unto you: There be some here of them that stand by which shall in no wise taste of death, till they see the kingdom of God come with power.*" This is not to be taken in a spiritual sense; it refers to the real Parousia. This will be in the lifetime of the present generation. But, this is the main point to be remarked here: Jesus does not say that all who stand around will be still alive. He solemnly declares: there will be some still alive when it happens to come. This looks rather like a later restriction made at a time when most of them who had been with Jesus had gone already without having seen His Parousia. But taken together with those other sayings it will prove to be the original conception of Jesus, explaining what He meant by generation, when He said: "*no sign to this generation*," and "*this generation shall not pass*" on the other side. We find a similar instance in the Old Testament—and we may suppose Jesus bearing this in mind—viz., that of all the generation which went out from Egypt only two, Joshua son of Nun, and Caleb son of Jephunneh, were able to enter the land of promise

(Num. xiv. 30, 38, cp. 1 Cor. x. 5). This parallel makes it quite clear that "*this generation*" is not to be taken in the sense of this nation (as some interpreters ventured to explain), but in the chronological sense of the word: the men just now living. This generation got the advantage of seeing God's highest revelation, compared with which even the time of the patriarchs and of Solomon counted for nothing; but having proved unworthy of such grace, this generation was to be called an evil and adulterous one. So it resulted that, while *the blood of all prophets would be required of this generation* (Luke xi. 51), or [in other words] *all these things would come upon this generation* (Matt. xxiii. 36), only few of them would be worthy to live to see the establishment of salvation, the coming of the Son of Man. It is indeed, as we said before, in Jesus' opinion, the last generation destined to see the kingdom of God.

This, I think, is not in contradiction with other sayings of Jesus: as, *e.g.*, His saying Mark xiii. 32 (cp. Matt. xxiv. 36): "*Of that day or that hour knoweth no one, not even the angels in heaven, neither the Son, but the Father,*" [1] because in putting the date at the end of His generation He gives no real date; nor by those two sayings dealing with the spread of the Gospel, viz., Matt. x. 23,

[1] It is an open question whether the words "*neither the Son*" are to be omitted in the text of Matthew or not. At all events they are genuine in Mark. And so the question can be only whether the omission is due to Matthew himself or to a later copyist, the motive being in both cases that the words seemed to be derogatory to the divinity of Christ.

"*Ye shall not have gone through the cities of Israel, till the Son of Man be come*"; and on the other side, Mark xiii. 10 (cp. Matt. xxiv. 14): "*The gospel must first be preached unto all nations,*" two statements contradicting one another and showing neither of them the genuine teaching of Jesus but the later views of Jewish and Gentile Christianity. Jesus' statement about the coming of the kingdom in the lifetime of His own generation is in full accordance with the general tenour of His admonitions. When He says, "*Watch therefore: for ye know not when the Lord of the house cometh*" (Mark xiii. 35; cp. Matt. xxiv. 42), He addresses, undoubtedly, the men of His own time, this and other parables having no effect if the Parousia was not supposed to occur in the lifetime of these men.

As a matter of fact He announces the

death of some of His disciples, *e.g.*, the sons of Zebedee (Mark x. 39; Matt. xx. 23) as well as He foretells His own death—I see no reason for treating this with Ed. Schwartz as an *ex eventu* prophecy—but this comes out rather as an exception, the disciples not being deprived by their martyrdom of the benefit of partaking in the glorious kingdom, no less than Jesus Himself, who firmly believed in getting through death to life, patronising in this department Pharisaic doctrine against Sadducean unbelief, or rather protecting by His own assent what was of real value in the progress of Jewish religious thought, at the same time improving it by putting out from it all sensuousness, all elements of worldly, chiliastic happiness: "*For when they shall rise from the dead, they neither marry, nor are given in marriage, but are as angels in heaven*" (Mark xii. 25 and par.).

In the same way, when Jesus speaks of a meal where the sons of the kingdom will be gathered with Abraham, Isaac, and Jacob, we may conclude that this is meant eschatologically, but not in a chiliastic sense as a big dinner, where—as it is represented sometimes in late Jewish literature, the Leviathan will be given as fish and the Behemoth as meat, and the cups will be filled with wine without end. As a matter of fact we find Jesus using the very words of being at table, eating bread and drinking the fruit of the vine in the kingdom of God (Matt. viii. 11; Luke xiii. 29, xiv. 15; Mark xiv. 25 c. par.); but here realistic interpretation is out of place; it is the popular way of expressing supreme happiness, which Jesus is using for something which is far beyond the literal sense of the words. Nobody I trust would imagine Jesus foretelling to His disciples the pleasures of a dinner in the Messianic kingdom, even when he takes the most realistic view of Jesus' eschatology.

Two more Features in the Genuine Jesus-Tradition

LECTURE III

TWO MORE FEATURES IN THE GENUINE JESUS-TRADITION

BY collecting and sifting the evidence afforded by our first three Gospels, we found that notwithstanding a marked tendency towards bringing in eschatological views there was a large enough genuine stock of eschatological sayings of Jesus to prove that He Himself believed in a change of all things which would come quickly, and not later than the end of His own generation; the kingdom of God would then be established in its full glory and happiness by

His own coming in power and glory; all His believers, or rather, all pious and good men, heathen as well as members of the chosen people, participating in its happy life. We do not see Jesus interested in the details of eschatology like most of the apocalyptic writers of late Judaism and early Christianity. For Jesus' eschatology has only a twofold significance: (1) it is a help for Him to understand and make men understand His own position: being the Messiah, the culmination in God's revelation to His people, final in all that He does and says, He brings about the kingdom of God; and (2) it is a motive in His admonitions: be ready, be watchful, because the kingdom of God is at hand.

I

But beside these clearly eschatological utterances there is another set of sayings dealing likewise with the notions of the kingdom and of His Messiahship, but showing quite a different aspect of them: the kingdom is present, and Jesus, humble and meek as He is, is the Messiah, because He fulfils the expectation in its true form and brings salvation in its deepest sense.

A. 1. When attacked on account of His casting out devils, Jesus argues—according to Mark iii. 24–27—by two parables: a kingdom divided against itself cannot stand, and a man cannot enter into a strong man's house and spoil his goods except he first binds the strong man. Q, represented by Luke xi. 19, 20 and Matthew xii. 27, 28, gives two more arguments used on the same occasion by Jesus. He refers to the casting out of devils by the rabbis and their pupils, so defending his own practice *per analogiam;* then He goes on to say: "*But if I by the finger* (or, according to Matthew, *by the spirit*) *of God cast out devils, then is the kingdom of God come upon you.*" This "*is come*" (ἔφθασε) must mean something more than the usual "*is at hand*" (ἤγγικεν); it is the solemn declaration that the kingdom is present in Jesus' acting; His casting out of devils proves that the powers of the kingdom are at work. Some interpreters take pleasure in urging the discrepancy between these two arguments. When Jesus' casting out of devils, they say, is nothing else than what was done by the rabbis, how can it be taken as a sign of the kingdom of God being present? Perhaps this is logically correct; it is hardly true psychologically; you can easily compare one thing with another without admitting that both are on the same level. That the casting out of devils by Jesus was far beyond the usual exorcism of the rabbis is admitted by His opponents by their very attack. If, then, the kingdom of God is proved to be present by the casting out of devils by Jesus, we have here a peculiar notion of the kingdom. There was, as we have seen before, beside the political notions of the kingdom of God, another idea in Jewish eschatology, a mythological one, taking the kingdom of God in contrast to the power of Satan and his evil spirits. This we have here; but the difference is that Jesus by His deeds realises the idea. He Himself is "the stronger," spoken of in that other parable connected with our saying both in Mark and Q, who, having first bound the strong man, spoils his goods. The individual act of casting out a devil is only the consequence of what Jesus has done before, overcoming Satan. So we read in Luke x. 18, that when the seventy returned with joy exulting that even the devils were subject to them in Jesus' name, Jesus answered them: "*I beheld Satan fallen as lightning from heaven.*" I am not prepared to accept this as a parallel to Revelation xii. 9, where the dragon is cast out from heaven and comes down to the earth in order to persecute the Children of the Church.[1] I understand it as an allegory of Satan's power being broken, so that it is easy work now to cast out his evil spirits. For the disciples

[1] F. Spitta, "Satan als Blitz" in Preuschen's *ZNTW*, ix., 1908, 160.

it is no matter of glorifying themselves on account of their exorcising power; they had rather enjoy their own salvation.

2. A second saying to be studied in this connexion is found in Luke xvii. 20–21 only: "*And being asked by the Pharisees, when the kingdom of God cometh, he answered them and said: the kingdom of God cometh not with observation, neither shall they say, Lo, here! or, There! for Lo, the kingdom of God is within you.*" So ἐντὸς ὑμῶν is translated both by the A.V. and the R.V., while some interpreters prefer to translate *in the midst of you.*[1] The discus-

[1] The Latin *intra vos* seems to patronise this later view: *unter euch, among you:* on Old Syriac *bainathchon* (*among you*) and Pešiṭṭa *begau menchon* (*in the midst of you*) and Diatessaron *within your heart,* see F. C. Burkitt, *Evangelion da Mepharreshe,* ii. 198,

sion as to the true meaning of this ἐντός goes through the whole history of interpretation and will perhaps never come to a final decision, most interpreters maintaining that there must be the same notion of presence as in the former saying. Joh. Weiss tries to get rid of this notion by taking "is in the midst of you" in the sense of "will then be in the midst of you suddenly, without being announced by outward visible preparations." But in order to express "in the midst of you" Luke would have used ἐμμέσῳ [1]; the rather uncommon expression ἐντὸς ὑμῶν he can have chosen only

298. A. Merx, *Die vier kanonischen Evangelien*, ii. 2, 347, understands the Pešiṭṭa meaning: "*within you*." "*Inside of you*" is the Bohairic rendering (G. Horner).

[1] This is found in Luke's writings more than a dozen times; ἐντός c. gen. only xvii. 21.

with the aim of giving to "*in*" the peculiar colouring of inwardness.[1] Now it may be an open question, if we can trust his rendering of the Aramaic original. There may have come in a misunderstanding in the very act of translation. But we cannot reach this Aramaic original behind the extant Greek text. And I see no necessity for putting aside Luke's meaning, as inwardness of the kingdom, if not stated expressly by other sayings of Jesus, is quite in the line of what he says about clean and unclean: "*There is*

[1] It is worth remark that the parallels brought forward in favour of the meaning "*in the midst of you*" are all taken from early writers, as Thukydides, Plato, Xenophon, whereas the LXX uses the word in the sense of "*in the interior of.*" I should attribute a great value, too, to the linguistic sensorium of Chrysostom, who champions the inward-view.

nothing from without the man, that going into him can defile him: but the things which proceed out of the man are those that defile the man;" "*for from within, out of the heart of men, evil thoughts proceed . . . and defile the man*" (Mark vii. 15, 21; cp. Matt. xv. 11, 19). If it is man's heart where the evil thoughts come from, or, in other words, where the devil exercises his dominion, then it is man's heart, too, where the kingdom of God is to be established. "*Thy kingdom come, thy will be done*" points in the same direction.

3. A third saying is still more difficult. It is found in Matt. xi. 12, 13, and Luke xvi. 16, *i.e.*, at two different places, and in two quite different forms, too. I therefore do not think that it comes from Q, but rather from some other source, perhaps an oral one. We hardly can say

what are the original words; we had better put the two redactions side by side:—

MATTHEW.	LUKE.
(*a*) And from the days of John the Baptist until now the kingdom of heaven suffereth violence, and men of violence[1] take it by force.	(*a*) The law and the prophets (were) until John:
(*b*) For all the prophets and the law prophesied until John.	(*b*) from that time the gospel of the kingdom of God is preached, and every man entereth violently[2] into it.

Whatever may be the original form (most of the interpreters trying to gain it by a rather hazardous combination);[3]

[1] The violent, A.V. [2] Presseth, A.V.

[3] See the various attempts at reconstruction by Wendt, *Lehre Jesu*, i. 75; Harnack, *Sprüche Jesu*, 101; B. Weiss, *Die Quellen der syn.*

whatever may be the meaning of that most disputed word βιασταί and βιάζεται (Luke, evidently taking the latter in a passive sense: *is compelled to enter into it*): one thing seems to be beyond any doubt: the time of Jesus is set in opposition to the time until John, the present to the past, and it is to this present that the kingdom of God belongs, not to a third form, the future. And because it is present, it is to be taken as something inward, some experience of happiness which men try to get so eagerly that they rather jostle one another in the effort to reach it.

4. A fourth saying, which one would mention in this connexion, is perhaps not so certain; it is found in Mark x. 15

Uberlieferung (*Texte u. Unters.*, 3 ser. ii. 3); H. von Soden, *Die wichtigsten Fragen in Leben Jesu*, does not include this saying in Q.

(cp. Luke xviii. 17 [1]): "*Verily I say unto you, Whosoever shall not receive the kingdom of God, as a little child, he shall in no wise enter therein.*" While in the second part the notion of the kingdom is the usual one, a different notion seems to be presupposed in the first part. If to receive the kingdom is the condition for entering into the kingdom, it must be in the first place some kingdom before the kingdom, *i.e.*, some inward experience, accessible to man in the present time, before the kingdom in the external eschatological sense is to be revealed. The kingdom of God as an experience of man's heart would be in agreement with what we learned from Luke xvii. 21. On the other hand, "*the kingdom of God*" can be taken here as

[1] Matthew omits this word at xix. 14, because he has a various form of the same in xviii. 3.

an abbreviated expression for the "gospel of the kingdom of God," and in this case the conclusion would not be quite necessary.

5. Lastly, we have to mention here the two parables of the mustard seed and the leaven, only the former being given in Mark iv. 30–32, while Luke xiii. 18–21, following probably Q, has the original couple, and Matthew xiii. 31–33 combines, as he likes to do, the Marcan form with the Q-tradition. The notion of the kingdom of God, given by these parables, is at any rate quite opposite to the eschatological one which makes the kingdom appear suddenly in its full power and glory. Here we are told that it is growing up, however quickly, and that it is exercising influence by its inheritant power. Certainly Jesus' opinion has nothing in common with the modern view of a gradual evolution, the seed of His gospel

coming to grow up by hundreds and hundreds of years. He thinks of a rapid growing up and a quick leavening of the whole people by His gospel. But at all events it is by His own preaching and teaching and healing that the kingdom is to be realised. We would not be surprised to hear Him speak of the great success of His gospel, as He tells His disciples in the parable of the sower that what falls into good ground brings fruit, some thirty and some sixty and some an hundred (Mark iv. 8). But in these two parables He is not speaking of His gospel, but of the kingdom of God, illustrating its extensive and intensive power. The conclusion is inevitable, that it is by His preaching that the kingdom comes, or, rather, is present; the effect of His preaching is that inward experience of man which we found identified with the notion of the kingdom in two former sayings.

B. This peculiar notion of the kingdom of God as some present, inward experience is supported by a set of sayings which show Jesus looking upon His own present activity as means of—not so much preparing, but bringing salvation to His people.

1. When the Baptist sends to Him asking, "*Art thou he that cometh, or look we for another?*" (Luke vii. 19, Matt. xi. 3), Jesus answers neither Yes nor No; He makes John glance over His activity and see how it fulfils what the prophets had said about the time of salvation. In whatever sense you may take the words, "*the blind receive their sight,*" &c., spiritual or realistic, Jesus' doings, His preaching, His healing fulfil these expectations. The Baptist, being a stern prophet of the last

judgment, had not done any miracle, as we are informed John x. 41[1]: Jesus is surrounded by miracles, the outward miracles of healing being, in His own opinion, only small proofs of the still greater inward miracles of conversion of sinners (Mark ii. 10 f.). So Jesus' answer to the Baptist is a Yes, but a Yes which has to be made out by the asking man himself: Look and see, and then you will make up your mind that I am really He that should come. Jesus, the humble Son of Man, the preaching and healing prophet, is indeed the Messiah. So He declares to the people by telling them that John the Baptist, the greatest of all prophets, is far behind any one who belongs to the

[1] The same is implied in the popular estimation of Jesus' relation to John, Mark vi. 14 (Matt. xiv. 2).

kingdom. He is not speaking of Himself, but whoever has ears to hear may understand that He who speaks is more than a small member of this kingdom: He is the king in this kingdom.

2. And His disciples did understand Him. At a time when the people still looked out for various solutions of the problem put before them by this Son of Man, who was so unlike all others, who, being the most humble and meek, yet spoke with power as nobody ever had spoken before Him; at a time when people called Him a prophet, one of the great prophets of times past, Elijah, or perhaps even John the Baptist himself, risen from death, and, therefore, gifted with miraculous power:—His disciples, by the mouth of Peter, found the right expression solemnly declaring Him to be the Messiah, *i.e.*, the unique, the final bringer

of salvation.[1] And He did not decline to be called so; He only forbade them to tell this to the people, because He was aware that such a claim would lead the people to expect of Him what He never intended to do, *i.e.*, to relieve the people from foreign tyranny, to deliver it from the Romans, and may be, even from the

[1] See Mark viii. 27 ff.; Matt. xvi. 13 ff.; Luke ix. 18 ff. There is an ingenious interpretation of the Lukan form by Prof. F. Spitta in his book *Streitfragen der Geschichte Jesu*, 1907, 85–843: ὑμεῖς δὲ τίνα με λέγετε εἶναι . . . τὸν Χριστὸν τοῦ θεοῦ, not being taken as the disciples' personal confession, but as their speaking to the people about Jesus (μηδενὶ λέγειν τοῦτο, ver. 21). Then the whole scene would have another significance than we are accustomed to; Mark must have misunderstood this, and Matthew reinforced this misinterpretation by his well-known addition. I am not convinced that this was Luke's meaning, nor that his relation is independent of Mark.

Sadducees; in one word, to carry on a line of political evolution. This He declined, and therefore He not only forbad His disciples to use the title of Messiah, but He told them at once that He had to be delivered into the hands of His enemies and to be put to death—death, however, not being able to destroy His work or overcome Himself.

3. Jesus' activity was indeed a Messianic one, if only we take this word not in its national and political sense, but in the purely religious meaning of bringing salvation and happiness. He said to His disciples, according to Luke x. 23 and Matt. xiii. 16: "*Blessed are the eyes which see the things which ye see, [and the ears which hear the things which ye hear]*:[1] *for*

[1] This part is wanting in Luke, but it is certainly original, as we have in Matt.:

I say unto you that many prophets and kings[1] *desired to see the things which ye see and saw them not, and to hear the things which ye hear and heard them not.*" We can hardly imagine a more solemn form of proclamation for the fact that in Christ's present actions all promises are fulfilled. And this is not the evangelists, Luke or Matthew, but it is Q or some other old source.

4. That in Jesus was fulfilled whatever was expected for the Messianic time, will further be seen by a comparison of several sayings:

a. A commonplace of eschatological ex-

"*Blessed are your eyes, for they see, and your ears, for they hear.*" The parallelism is supported also by the continuation.

[1] The "*righteous men*" of Matthew is probably his own; he likes this combination, cp. x. 41, xxiii. 29.

pectation was mutual hatred between the nearest relations. So Mark xiii. 12 (cp. Luke xxi. 16; Matt. x. 21, xxiv. 10) records as a saying of Jesus that in the last time *brother shall deliver up brother to death and the father his child, and children shall rise up against parents, and cause them to be put to death.* Now in Q we read nearly the same, but it runs quite another way, Jesus saying—

LUKE xii. 51–53.	MATTHEW x. 34–35.
Think ye that I am come to give peace in the earth? I tell you, Nay, but rather division: for there shall be from henceforth five in one house divided, three against two, and two against three. They	Think not that I came to send peace on the earth; I came not to send peace but a sword. For I came to set a man at variance against his father, and the daughter against her mother, and the

shall be divided, father against son and son against the father, mother against daughter and daughter against her mother; mother-in-law against her daughter-in-law and daughter-in-law against her mother-in-law.

daughter-in-law against her mother-in-law.

Jesus is come to fulfil what was expected for the last time. And Jesus Himself realises some of this result of His mission by the unbelief He met with in His own family (Mark iii. 21, 31 ff.; cp. Matt. xii. 46 ff., Luke viii. 19 ff., John vii. 5), and on the part of his countrymen (Mark vi. 1–6; cp. Matt. xiii. 53–58, Luke iv. 16–30).

b. The Messianic judgment was to bring up a sharp separation, as is said in a saying recorded by Q itself: "*Then shall two men be in the field* (or according to Luke:

"*In that night there shall be two men on one bed*), *one is taken and one is left; two women shall be grinding at the mill, one is taken and one is left*" (Matt. xxiv. 40, 41; Luke xvii. 34). Now this very separation is worked out by Jesus Himself when He calls some fishermen to follow Him and left others; when He calls Levi and Zacchaeus the publicans and the Pharisees stand outside; when He declines to allow the one who asks to follow Him, whereas He presses on another who is rather unwilling: "*follow me; and leave the dead to bury their own dead*" (Matt. viii. 22; Luke ix. 60).

c. At the Messianic time a large festival was expected, all members of the chosen people taking part in it. Jesus, in His well-known parables accepts this expectation correcting only its last part. Those who were first invited refusing to come, others will be introduced (Luke xiv. 16–24; Matt. xxii. 1–14); this is nearly the same as what He says about the heathen taking a place at the Messianic table together with the patriarchs (Luke xiii. 28 ff.; Matthew viii. 11 f.). But the same is fulfilled already in Jesus' own lifetime by His preaching the gospel of the kingdom to the poor, declaring that the publicans and harlots go into the kingdom of God before the Pharisees (Matt. xxi. 31 f.; cp. Luke vii. 29); it is accomplished when He sits down with publicans and sinners, so that the honourable men who pretend to be alone worthy of His company are rather shocked (Mark ii. 15 f. c. par.); when he finds faith among Gentiles in a measure He never had found before among His own countrymen (Luke vii. 9; Matt. viii. 10).

5. All this points to the same effect: Jesus is the Messiah, whatever may be the

discrepancy between His appearance and the popular expectation. He is the Messiah in this sense, that He brings judgment and salvation. He is the stumbling-block for one class of men, and to the other He brings happiness and joyous life. As He is the son, so His disciples are the son, freed from all bondship, so that they need not even pay the regular tax for the temple, a saying which, though found only in Matthew xvii. 26, in a context belonging to a not very trustworthy collection of Peter stories, nevertheless has a genuine colouring.

Jesus as surrounded by His disciples represents the new era of Messianic time. The wedding, a very common Messianic notion, spoken of in so many parables of Jesus, is already going on; Jesus is the bridegroom, His disciples are the children of the bride-chamber, as He puts it in His apology for non-fasting (Mark ii. 19, 20;

cp. Matt. ix. 15, Luke v. 34, 35). This is all the more remarkable as we have it not in Q as most of the words mentioned before, but in that same Marcan tradition which we found to be distinguished for its eschatological views.[1] Jesus looked upon His estate as belonging already to the new order of things. So in the parables of the piece of new cloth and of the new wine (combined in Mark ii. 21, 22, c. par. with

[1] About the authenticity there can be no doubt (against Wellhausen). The question rather is, if those words belong to so early a period in the life of Jesus (Wendt). As a matter of fact, Mark's chronological arrangement is not beyond doubt; it was criticised already by the Elder from whom Papias got his information. But having no means of settling the chronological order by ourselves, we had better refrain from expressing decision. I am not persuaded that there was an evolution in Jesus' thought during His public ministry.

the parable of the bridegroom) He declares as clearly as possible, that there is something new about Him in opposition to all that which was before. It is the same contrast as we found it in the word Luke xvi. 16, dealing with John the Baptist as representative of the time gone and the preaching of the kingdom as the characteristic of the time now.

Here we may stop. The evidence collected is quite sufficient to prove that in the teaching of Jesus there is a strong line of what I would call *transmuted eschatology.* I mean eschatology transmuted in the sense that what was spoken of in Jewish eschatology as to come in the last days is taken here as already at hand in the lifetime of Jesus; transmuted at the same time in the other sense that what was expected as an external change is taken inwardly: not all people seeing it, but Jesus' disciples becoming aware of it. For the great mass of the people Jesus is only one of the prophets; for His enemies, Pharisees as well as Sadducees, He is a pseudo-prophet deceiving the people; but His disciples recognise and acknowledge Him to be the Messiah, the Chosen one of God; and in His company they enjoy all the happiness of the Messianic time.

Now we must compare this with the first group of sayings dealing with pure eschatology: Jesus the Messiah to come on the clouds of heaven; the Messianic judgment to be held at the end of the days; the Messianic meal to take place after this glorious event, and so on. Both groups are quite distinct and to be kept separate. Neither of them may be reduced easily to the other one without violence being done to the tradition, nor can we put aside one of them as a later addition or transformation, both being attested by our best sources. One may say that in Mark the eschatological view prevails, whereas the other view is predominant in Q; but Q is not without eschatology, nor Mark without the other element. This is the evidence of the Gospel-tradition.

II

Before starting a solution of this problem, we have to take account of one more point of tradition, worth being remarked.

Taking together all materials collected hitherto, eschatology as well as transmuted eschatology, we find that they represent only a small part of the whole Gospel-tradition; there are plenty of sayings beside these, which we may call, for the sake of brevity, entirely non-eschatological. We do not need lose time with a detailed investigation, Every one knows what Jesus says about trust in God, God's care for the individual, about prayer and the certainty of its being heard, not trusting in riches, loving the neighbour and even the enemy, pardoning offenders, &c. It is (as Harnack stated against Wellhausen) the great value of Q that it represents Jesus from this peculiar side. But even in Mark we have plenty of this non-eschatological, purely moral matter: *e.g.*, Jesus' sayings about cleanness (vii. 1–23), marriage and divorce (x. 1–12), children (x. 13–16), and the rich (x. 17–31). It may be interesting to settle this statement by means of a peculiar inductive investigation.

There are the so-called doublets, *i.e.*, sayings related both by Mark and Q. They are of some importance in the critical study of the Gospels, some critics maintaining that they prove a literary relation to exist between these two main sources—I on the contrary, am rather inclined to say that they prove both sources to be independent, giving the same saying mostly in quite different renderings. But they have another importance, too, as Professor Burkitt has pointed out [1]: they allow us to infer not only which sayings are the best attested, but at the same time sayings which were the most appreciated, and, therefore, had the widest circulation and the greatest influence. Now out of the thirty doublets, which may be read in

[1] *The Gospel History and its Transmission*, 1906, 147 ff. Cp. also Sir John Hawkins, *Horae Synopticae*, 1899, 65 ff., and Professor V. H. Stanton, *The Gospels as Historical Documents*, ii., 1909, 59–60.

Professor Burkitt's book there are but seven dealing with eschatology,[1] all the others containing non-eschatological matter of a moral character. Of course the eschatological background may give a peculiar colouring to some of them; *e.g.*, that *nothing is hid save that it should be manifested*, may, set by itself, well be taken as an announcement of the last judgment. But, in general, we should not miss anything for the understanding of those general moralisations, if we had no knowledge of the eschatology of Jesus.

At this point we may be able to pronounce a fair criticism of the so-called theory of "consistent eschatology." According to this theory there is nothing

[1] Nos. 2, 3, 12, 15, 29, 30, 31 in Burkitt's list.

in the life of Jesus nor in His sayings which is not to be explained by eschatology, that is to say, by Jesus' belief that He was to bring the end of this present order of things. Now (1) this theory is to be maintained only by doing violence to the tradition, which, besides some distinct eschatological matter, gives a few but very expressive instances of what I have called transmuted eschatology, and as the main content a large amount of non-eschatological matters. It means doing violence to Jesus' moral teaching, if this is subordinated to His announcement of the approaching end in the way of being only an "Interimsethik"; it means doing violence to the other group of sayings representing the kingdom and the Messiahship as present, if these are taken only as mere anticipations of the future, to be jumped over, while Jesus' real doctrine is said to be represented only by the first group of sayings, the purely eschatological group. (2) The surprising lights this theory seems to throw upon several points of the gospel history are gained by a strange interpretation which reads into the text what is to be demonstrated: *e.g.*, when the feeding of the multitude as well as the last supper is taken as a Messianic sacrament, assuring to all partakers the participation at the Messianic meal, it has to be admitted that there is not the slightest indication thereof in the texts, but even that probably no one of all who were present was able to conceive this meaning. (3) It is Jesus Himself who contradicts this modern view of His activity, viz., that He was working by all His forces to the effect of bringing about the kingdom of God or the end of history; in the parable of the seed

(Mark iv. 26–29) he expressly states that when the seed has been cast into the ground the man has nothing else to do but to wait for the time of harvest.

It is not only the amount of non-eschatological materials in the Gospels that forbids us to account for Jesus' whole life and teaching by His eschatology. It is at the same time the permanent value of His non-eschatological doctrines that causes us to put them in the first rank, whereas the transmuted eschatology points out in what direction Jesus Himself would form the mind of His believers. It is, lastly, as we have said before, the history of the Christian Church, from its beginning in the apostolic age to our own time, that proves the non-eschatological element to be essential. This statement does not include, however, the opposite thesis, that eschatology has no place at all in Jesus' mind. A sound and sober interpretation will be found to be one which gives to every group of sayings its own value and weight.

Jesus
Various Modes of Understanding (St. John)

LECTURE IV

JESUS. VARIOUS MODES OF UNDERSTANDING (ST. JOHN).

OUR investigation of the Gospel-tradition led us to the conclusion that there are different lines of thought, and various groups of sayings, which have each of them the same claim to be accounted for, if we try to make out what was Jesus' own opinion. We will do our best to combine them in a way of a psychological analysis of the leading ideas in Jesus. Contrary to the order of our former investigation, we will begin with the third group of sayings, *i.e.*, the non-eschatological group, which we found to cover the most space and to be of the highest importance.

(*a*) Jesus, as it is commonly said, started as a teacher of piety and morality. So at least people understood Him. They called Him a rabbi, remarking, however, that there was something in Him far above the doctrine of the rabbis of His time. It has been proclaimed by many a rationalistic writer of recent time, and especially by modern Jewish authorities, that Jesus was nothing but a reformer of moral ideas, and that He did not go beyond the line of the best moralists of His time, such as, *e.g.*, Rabbi Hillel. There are coincidences, of course, for Hillel also summed up the whole of the law in one sentence, the so-called golden rule. But we need only read attentively Jesus' explanation of the law as given in Matt. v.

to see the difference. He expresses not an individual opinion which may be balanced by the authority of some other rabbi—the way in which the rabbinical schools of that time used to settle questions concerning the law—but gives *the* explanation; He fulfils the law, as it is said, by setting finally the rule which is to guide its interpretation. He even speaks with no less authority than the law itself: "*You have heard that it was said to them of old time: but I say unto you,*" and sometimes He sets aside the letter of the law by giving higher ordinances of His own, as in the law of the Sabbath, the law of purification, the law of divorce, &c.

There are others who consider Him more than a rabbi, and are prepared to acknowledge that His teaching is rather to be compared with the teaching of the great prophets of a former time, the prophets whose great work was to raise the religion of Israel to a higher platform of ethical conceptions. Jesus, it has been said, overcame the rabbinical Judaism of His time, with all its ritualistic and legalistic moralities, by going back to the simple and lofty standard of the old prophets. There is undoubtedly some truth in this statement. We need only read Mark vii. or x. to see how deeply Jesus' mind was filled with prophetical sayings, how He opposed Old Testament authority to the traditional doctrine of the rabbis of His time. But this touches only the form of His utterances, and you will remark that while the prophet is speaking in the name of his God, Jesus sets His own authority even against the Divine Law. There is something more in His teaching than a mere restoration of the old prophetical religion.

In the last twenty years there has been a great change as regards Jesus' teaching —or rather, our view of religion has been changed by rediscovering that morals, however important in religion, are not *the* religion, that there is a religion something beyond all that is moral, intellectual, æsthetic, some real intercourse with God. We may call this mysticism, only that it is not necessarily mysticism in the strict sense of the word with a naturalistic notion about Deity as its basis and including some materialistic means of intercourse with the Divine. In Judaism, certainly, this element of nature-religion had been cast away long before, and it came into Christianity only later through pagan influence. It marks the position of Jesus in the history of religion, that He is the culmination of that line of religion which has broken off all relation to the primitive cult of nature and has put in its place the idea of God's moral holiness, and that to do the will of God makes the man religious. But, as we have remarked already, to do the will of God is not in itself the religion, but a part of it, or, rather, a consequence of it. The centre of religion is a real experience of God's presence and helpfulness, of His grace and mercy. And this is what we find in complete fulness in Jesus. It is only by taking account of this fundamental part of Jesus' doctrine, that we can hope to approach His own meaning as well as His position in the history of mankind. Jesus' teaching deals not so much with morals, however important the moral element of His teaching may be: He preaches a new relation of God to man and of man to God; or better, He brings, He represents this new relation. And this is, we may say confidently, what constitutes His distinction from, and His superiority to all prophets. He has in Himself the unity with God which He brings to mankind. He does not only tell how to realise a new form of relation to God; He embodies it in Himself.

(*b*) Now, without entering into the profound question of metaphysical speculation, we may simply say that Jesus, according to His own words, felt this relation to God to be unique in Himself, and that He had no other means of explaining it and speaking about it than by calling God His Father and Himself God's Son. We may be sure He supposed that the same relation ought to exist between God and every one else. But His refined moral sense must have discovered at a very early period of His life the difference between Himself and others in this respect, He Himself being in uninterrupted communion with His Father, while all others were separated from God by sin. He felt the longer, the more that it was His task to bring them into full communion with God. His life was to be devoted to this very aim, to remove all that could stand between God and mankind.

This is, I should think, the real meaning of what we call Jesus' "*Tauferlebnis*," the experience at the moment of His baptism: He became aware of this as the task laid upon Him by His Father's will. This, at the same time, explains the story of the temptation, that in taking upon Him that task, He had to come to terms with the ordinary Messianic notion of His people. "*Thou art My beloved Son, in Thee I am well pleased.*" This Jesus had known all His life; but at this very moment it gained a new significance for Him. He was to be the Son of God, acknowledged as such by His people; in other words, He was to be the Messiah.[1] Of course, Jesus did not think of Himself as the Messiah according to the current popular notion; this He declined, as we learn from the story of the temptation. Whatever may be the kernel of this story, it shows that it is a mistake, in order to get at a solution of the problem, to start from the current popular notion and ask how Jesus could adopt this. The late Professor A. Merx (of Heidelberg) was quite right in denying that Jesus ever thought of adopting this.[2] We have to go the opposite way: we take it for granted that Jesus had a peculiar estimation of His own importance, what German theology

[1] Cp. on this topic E. Schürer, *Das messianische Selbstbewusstsein Jesu*, Göttingen, 1903.

[2] *Die vier kanonischen Evangelien*, ii. 1, 1902, 186 and *passim*.

calls his "*Selbstbewusstsein.*" Conscious as He was of a unique position involving a great task as well as a supreme authority, He had no other notion in the language of His people to describe this position than that of Messiah. Rabbi was a common title, expressing the human authority of scholarship, a man of letters, a man who studies and knows the law. Jesus was no man of letters: He of course knew the law, but not by scholarly training; He knew it as the will of His Father. He was far above all that could be meant by calling Him a rabbi. Nor would prophet have been sufficient to express His own self-appreciation; there had been prophets in great number: He knew His position was unique; the prophets had all been talking about a time of fulfilment to come: He was bringing this time. They all derived their authority from a special calling, from individual acts of inspiration: He did not need such calling; His understanding of God His Father was beyond all inspiration. So to express His unique position there was no other means than to adopt the title of Messiah, and to express His task there was no other way than to preach the kingdom of God, because the Messiah was to bring salvation, and the kingdom of God was the most comprehensive term for final salvation. Both notions undoubtedly included at that time many other things. So it has been said, with some appearance of truth, that Jesus, when adopting such terms in a sense different from the current one, was bound to give at the beginning of His teaching a clear statement about His own understanding of it. As He did not do so, He must, we are told, have taken the notions in their current sense, and we are bound to accept them in the realistic meaning of late Jewish eschatology. I do not think the presuppositions are right: Jesus was not a philosopher proceeding upon definitions and conclusions. He was a preacher, or rather, His way was preaching. And we see Him going on slowly in His declarations. He likes to make men find out by themselves what He is. You remember His answer to the Baptist. He likes to put forth things in such a way that they are clear for those who are willing to understand, whereas others may guess as they like. Mark is surely not quite wrong in his statement regarding the parabolic form of Jesus' teaching—parables including indeed, besides their proper aim of illustrating, some element of concealment. So it is easy enough to explain how the Messiahship of Jesus came to be looked upon by His disciples as a mystery not to be revealed to the people. There is no necessity for accepting the ingenious, but rather too ingenious, theory of the late Professor W. Wrede (of Breslau),[1] who maintained this conception of a mystery to involve the implicit confession that at a later time two opposite views were combined, viz., an earlier view regarding Jesus as Messiah only after His death and resurrection, and a later one taking Him as Messiah already in His lifetime.

As an example of Jesus' own way of dealing with His Messiahship, let us take His entrance into Jerusalem, which usually is declared to be the most solemn form of Messianic self-declaration. But where is the Messianic element? To ride upon

[1] *Das Messiasgeheimnis in den Evangelien*, 1901.

an ass is a very common fashion, occurring frequently in Talmudic narratives regarding celebrated rabbis. The devotion of His adherents in breaking branches from the trees and putting their garments in the way, is not so extraordinary in eastern lands as it may seem to western readers. Even the shouting, "*Hosanna! Blessed He who comes in the name of the Lord,*" is not by itself a clear statement of Messiahship, for Matthew, as a matter of fact, says that the people declared Jesus to be the prophet from Galilee (xxi. 11). So His entrance was not interpreted as a royal one, as a solemn declaration of Messianic dignity. I quite agree that Jesus Himself meant to enter the capital of His people as the Messiah, and that by riding on an ass He intended to make allusion to the prophecy of Zechariah; but the manner He chose for His entrance was very fit for declaring His Messianic dignity to those who were able and inclined to understand and to conceal it from the others. Whatever one may think of this behaviour, I am sure there is no other means of explaining the tradition. Jesus goes His way in the full consciousness of His unique position; but while others would have spoken of their mission in the highest terms, He only preaches the kingdom of God, and chooses for Himself the lowest of all Messianic titles—a title not even regarded as involving Messiahship by the mass of the people. He does His work, and He leaves it to His Father to reveal His Son to mankind. This He tells us in that famous saying called usually, according to Luke's introduction, "the Agalliasis" (Luke x. 21, 22; Matt. xi. 25, 27). Jesus is the Messiah. However slow may be the understanding of His claim on the part of His disciples, He is the Messiah from the very beginning of His public career, and not only, as has been said recently,[1] from the time of His transfiguration. This transfiguration has significance not for Himself but for His disciples, the heavenly voice being not a declaration on the part of the Father to the Son, like that at the baptism, "*Thou art My beloved Son, in whom I am well pleased*," but rather a declaration to the witnesses on behalf of the Son, "*This is My beloved Son: hear ye Him*" (Mark ix. 7).[2]

[1] Harnack, *Sprüche Jesu*, 138, n. 1.

[2] Harnack (*l.c.* 172_2) is quite right insisting upon the priority of the *Sohnesbewusstsein* compared with the *Messiasbewusstsein;* but these two steps in the evolution of Jesus' self-consciousness correspond to the period before his public

Jesus not only preaches the kingdom of heaven, He brings it by casting out devils and forgiving sins, by healing diseases and filling men with a new spirit, by spreading around Himself an atmosphere of happiness and salvation. Whoever enjoys in company with Him His complete communion with God, belongs to the kingdom and gets all its blessings.

All this belongs to what we called the transmuted eschatology; this best expresses Jesus' proper view. The second group of sayings, however small it may be, is the most conspicuous: Jesus the Messiah, *i.e.*, the Saviour bringing actual and present salvation to all those who follow Him, salvation indeed in a purely

ministry and during it, not to two parts of His public life.

religious and moral sense, very different from what people expected: "*Blessed are ye poor, for yours is the kingdom of God.*"

(*c*) There still remains the first group of purely eschatological sayings, and we have now to try to make out their significance for Jesus Himself and His disciples. Thinking of Jesus as a teacher of systematic theology, one would be inclined to say: Granted that Jesus was persuaded that He was the Messiah in the true religious sense of the word and brought salvation to His people, there was no need of talking about a future kingdom of God or of a coming again in the clouds of heaven. These are notions belonging to a former stage of religious insight, and corrected and overthrown by Jesus' own new views. Transmuted eschatology makes eschatology an unnecessary and even wrong supposition. So one could argue; but I do not think that this is right. Jesus, looking upon the misunderstanding and even hatred with which He met, could not think of His actual work as being the final establishment of God's kingdom. Jesus reading the Holy Scriptures could not help acknowledging that the prophecies wanted some other fulfilment. Being convinced that He was the Messiah, and that He was bringing salvation to His people and all mankind, He had to look forward to a final success, and it was only in the forms given by the prophets of old and by the apocalyptic tradition that He could imagine it. Being sure that He represented in Himself the culmination of the religious history of His people, He could only think of Himself, trained as He was in Jewish views, as standing at the end of history, at the meeting-point of the two ages. Thus His coming back with the clouds of heaven in the glory of the Father and the holy angels must needs occur in a very short time. This, I think, is the way in which one may easily explain how Jesus came to accept the eschatological views of His time. Conservative as He was, I think this was only natural for Him (if we are allowed to apply psychology to so exceptional a case). He did but add eschatological expectation to His conviction of being already in an eschatological relationship to the world, the term being understood in the transmuted sense. It was an inevitable consequence of His trust in God His Father. God could not leave His work undone or only half done. He would certainly bring it to a plain issue. He was bound to fulfil all His promises. Salvation, as brought by Jesus, was only an individual and inward experience; it ought to be some collective and outward fact. It is, as we have seen, characteristic of Jesus' eschatological teaching, that He makes no efforts to get a more detailed view of eschatology; He confines Himself to repeating the outlines of what was given by prophetic and apocalyptic tradition, emphasising only two points, viz., the responsibility of men regarding the coming judgment and that He Himself is the Son of Man, who will pronounce judgment. As He expressly says about the time, that no one, not even the Son, but only the Father knows it, so He leaves to the Father also the form in which all that is to be expected will be fulfilled. He only expresses His own opinion that it will happen soon, so that men must be prepared, and that it will be glorious, so that He Himself will be justified even in the eyes of His enemies, who condemned Him to death.

If we take it in this fashion, we shall easily come to a fair understanding. And we shall, I think, discover at the same time how to deal with the difficult question whether Jesus was misled in His expectation.

In fact, He did not come back in the clouds of heaven in the lifetime of His own generation. He has not come yet. The history of the world did not come to an end soon after mankind reached its highest religious level in Jesus; it has continued through many centuries, going up and down, mankind falling back to a lower standard and climbing again, but never reaching the height represented in Jesus. So He was wrong in His expectation. Was He really? If we keep to the letter of His words, we cannot help agreeing that He was wrong regarding the outward form of His predictions, and especially the time of God's fulfilment. But this does not involve, I am sure, any imperfection on His side, any more than His opinion about the sun as a star going around the earth, or about the Pentateuch as a book written by Moses. In all these respects He was a Jew of His time. But as we have remarked already, the form of His expectation was unimportant even for Himself. He left it to His Father how and when He would realise it. His belief was that His work and His own person could not be overthrown, that His work, confined as it was to a small circle, should gain universal importance and undisputed success, and that He Himself should be acknowledged by every man as what He was: the king of the kingdom of God.

Now in this expectation He was not wrong. His work has gone on through His death and resurrection in a wonderful way: the Church founded by His disciples upon belief in His name, has spread through the world, and will—so we hope—gain the whole earth. He Himself is acknowledged and adored as the Son of God by millions and millions of believers. Looking back through history, we may see His work in the judgment upon His nation, the Holy City being destroyed and the nation scattered over the world. So far Luke's interpretation is right; only it is the view of a later time looking upon Jesus' prophecies in the light of a fulfilment, which even He Himself did not imagine. We may truly say that it pleased God to fulfil Jesus' words thus, but we would be guilty of false witness if we dared to maintain that Jesus

Himself expressed this as His own opinion.

II

Beside this historical *ex eventu* interpretation, there is another, which is regarded by many a pious Christian as the true one. I mean the interpretation given to the eschatological sayings in the Fourth Gospel. I have avoided up till now making use of this Gospel, the reason for which will be seen presently. Our research, however, would not be complete if we did not at least glance at it.

As a specimen I select two passages dealing with Jesus' coming (xiv. 15–29), and with the judgment (v. 19–29), two notions of undoubted eschatological origin.

(*a*) It is rather hard to say what the coming in chap. xiv. may be meant to be. As the sayings concerning this idea are placed now between other sayings dealing with the coming of the Comforter, one would feel inclined to say: it is Jesus coming by His Spirit; it is at Pentecost that this promise was fulfilled. But there is evidently some distinction between the sending of the Comforter and the coming of Jesus Himself. When we compare chap. xvi. *v.* 16, "*A little while, and ye behold Me no more* (*ye shall not see Me*, A.V.), *and again a little while, and ye shall see Me*," we feel compelled to think of the appearances of the risen Lord. And this would suit very well the question of that other Judas (chap. xiv. *v.* 22): "*Lord, what is come to pass that Thou wilt manifest Thyself unto us, and not unto the world?*" The risen Lord appeared, as has been remarked from the earliest time, only to His believers, and the Greek used here, ἐμφανίζειν ἑαυτόν, is a technical term for appearances of healing gods who come to visit these adherents in dreams. But let us look more closely at the two verses, xvi. 16 and xiv. 19, and it will appear that there is a marked difference. The former, "*A little while, and ye behold Me no more, and again a little while, and ye see Me,*" has certainly to do with death and resurrection. But the latter in the passage before us, "*Yet a little while, and the world beholdeth Me no more, but ye behold Me; because I live, < and > ye shall live also,*" runs quite differently. It is the abiding communion of the Lord with His disciples, unbroken even by death, which finds here a splendid exposition. That this is the true meaning will be seen by the answer given to Judas: "*If a man love Me, he will keep My* *word, and My Father will love him, and* WE *will come unto him and make our abode with him.*" It is impossible not to see that this means nothing else than an inward dwelling of God and of the Lord in the hearts of Christians, what we may call mystical union, although St. John understands it rather in an ethical than in a mystical way. Even this idea of an indwelling God can be traced back to an eschatological conception, found in the Old Testament prophets: God abiding in the midst of His people, either in the temple of His Holy City, or perhaps, as it is put in the Christian apocalypse, instead of the temple. There is no need of sunlight, God Himself being in their midst. But you will easily observe how much this is altered. There is no more eschatology; its place has been taken by mysticism; the nation has given place to the individual. Instead of dwelling in the midst of His people, God is dwelling inwardly in the hearts of the individual believers. Now when we ask, Is this Jesus or is it a Johannine conception, one may at first sight be inclined to think of it as a genuine utterance of the Lord. It is very like what we have called transmuted eschatology. I need only remind you of our interpretation of the word ἐντός ὑμῶν (Luke xvii. 21), which we found to represent Jesus' own teaching, that the kingdom is "within you," *i.e.*, something inward, an experience of the heart, a rule governing man's will. But—we must remark the very important difference—it is the kingdom of God which is here spoken of, not God or Jesus; it is a purely ethical inwardness, expressed by these words, while there is some mystical element in the words as given by the Fourth Gospel, personal union between God and man, Jesus and man. And this is not an original view of Jesus: it is, however, what we find in St. John elsewhere. We need only compare Revelation iii. 20: "*Behold, I stand at the door and knock: if any man hear My voice and open the door, I will come in to him, and will sup with him, and he with Me.*" It is the well-known eschatological notion of a Messianic supper, where all the saints will be at table with the Son of Man and the patriarchs. Only it is not said here, "He who hears My voice shall enter into the wedding and sit down at My table," but, "I will come in to him and will sup with him." It is again an inward and individual experience instead of an outward and collective fact; the eschatological picture is turned into some mystical idea. Here we have the Johannine conception as we found it in the Gospel. So I venture to say: The coming of the Lord promised by Himself as an outward eschatological act is changed into an inward mystical experience by this Johannine colouring of His words. I quite agree that there is some connexion with one line of Jesus' thoughts. His conception of the ethical inwardness of religion reacted upon the eschatological ideas, and out of this combination there arose what we rightly may call the Johannine mysticism. Only, in order to understand this process thoroughly, we must remember that it was not in Palestine but in Asia Minor that St. John—whoever he was—lived; that he was surrounded by a Hellenistic atmosphere; and that this, full of mysticism, helped to transform his Jewish conceptions. The ethical inwardness of Jesus and the mysticism of Hellenistic religion had to co-operate in order to produce this change of attitude. So it happened that the idea of the Parousia was turned into the idea of Jesus coming into the hearts of His believers.

This interpretation, however, does not account for the whole passage we are dealing with. We do not reach the full meaning of its content if we confine ourselves to this mystical colouring of the original eschatological conception. There is another element in it, which we may call an historical adaptation: the coming of Jesus is understood as meaning the appearances of the risen Lord. This at least is the meaning of some words in these chapters, as we have seen before, the promises of Jesus that He would come again being interpreted from the experiences of the earliest Christianity as fulfilled in the appearances of the risen Lord.

Another experience was the coming of the Holy Ghost, and this led to the juxtaposition of the sayings regarding the Comforter with the sayings about Jesus' own coming, with the result that the latter may now be understood as identical with the former.

So we may rightly distinguish a triple stratification: (1) the underlying eschatological one, representing Jesus' own view; (2) the mystical one, which we may call the main Johannine stratum; and (3) a twofold historical adaptation: Jesus' coming is to be seen in His appearances or in His sending the Comforter; both these adaptations may be attributed to a later stage of Johannine thought, represented by the author of the Fourth Gospel, whom I believe to have been a pupil of John the Presbyter, the Elder of Ephesus.

(*b*) The other passage which I choose as an illustration is found in chap. v. *vv.* 19–29. This passage deals with resurrection and judgment, two notions which undoubtedly belong to the eschatological stock of late Jewish doctrines, and are found in Jesus' teaching in their original meaning. But here in the Fourth Gospel we have them coloured almost to an opposite meaning. Except the last two verses, the passage in question deals entirely with the spiritual experiences of Christianity. The judgment—or, as I would prefer to translate, the discrimination—between good and bad happens not at the end of the world, but, as it is said in chap. iii. *vv.* 18–21, when Jesus preaches (or the gospel is preached) and one man believes and the other refuses.

This is what the Fourth Gospel calls the judgment, a self-going-on process, an automatic judgment upon the moral work of men: those who do well will be attracted by the light of the gospel, those who do badly will withdraw from this light. And so their fate will be decided without any special judgment having to be pronounced on the part of God. This is called ἡ κρίσις, *the judgment* (R.V.), or, as the Authorised Version has it, *the condemnation.* So it is said: "*He that heareth My word, and believeth Him that sent Me, hath eternal life, and cometh not into judgment but hath passed out of death into life*" (or, *is passed from death unto life*, A.V.). This gives the old notion of resurrection, but changed into something inward, so that it reminds us of the teaching of the Gnostics, as given by the Pastoral Epistles, that the resurrection has already taken place (ἀνάστασιν ἤδη γεγονέναι, 2 Tim. ii. 18). This spiritualising tendency of Johannine teaching is best seen in chap. v. *v.* 25, "*Verily, verily, I say unto you, the hour cometh, and now is, when the dead shall hear the voice of the Son of God, and they that hear shall live.*" This sounds purely eschatological, very like the description of the great act of resurrection as we find it *e.g.* in St. Paul's first letter to the Thessalonians (iv. 16), "*For the Lord Himself shall descend from heaven, with a shout, with the voice of the archangel, and with the trump of God: and the dead in Christ shall rise first.*" But as it stands in John v. it cannot be taken in this eschatological sense, but only in a spiritual one: the dead are men dead in their sin; the voice of the Son of God is the preaching of Jesus; not all are listening to it, only some hear it, *i.e.*

credit Him, believe in Him; those who believe gain life, not only a life of future time, but life in the full sense of the word, presently.

This meaning here is unmistakable. But the Fourth Gospel does not stop here; it goes on supplementing the inward spiritual view by an outward eschatological outlook, and thereby distinguishing Johannine theology from the doctrine of Gnostic heretics. We read nearly the same words again, only a few verses later on, *v.* 28, 29, but now in a clear eschatological form: "*Marvel not at this; for the hour cometh, in which all that are in the tombs shall hear His voice, and shall come forth, they that have done good, unto the resurrection of life, and they that have done ill, unto the resurrection of judgment*" (or better, *damnation*, A.V.). It is quite clear: these verses are dealing with some future event—there is no word about the hour being now, as in *v.* 25; they speak of a general resurrection—there is no distinction between those who hear and those who do not hear; they indicate a bodily resurrection—"*all that are in the tombs*" is not susceptible of a spiritual interpretation as "*the dead*" of *v.* 25. There are two different notions of life expressed in these two verses: inward, present, spiritual; and external, future, in one word, eschatological. Chap. v. *vv.* 28, 29 gives indeed the description of what is called in Revelation xx. 7–15 the second resurrection, only that which precedes in *v.* 25 does not correspond to the first resurrection in Revelation xx. 1–6. It is not so much a first and a second resurrection as a regeneration and then a resurrection. Of course, *vv.* 28, 29, as they are put now, are meant to be an explanatory repetition, a corroboration and at the same time an interpretation of *v.* 25. But taken in their proper sense, they deal with two quite different notions and originate in different conceptions; *vv.* 28, 29 give the current popular eschatology in its realistic form, which has been transmuted by spiritualising in *v.* 25. The curious phenomenon here is that the transmuted eschatology appears as the main line, the underlying popular eschatology only as an additional feature.

Now this comes very near to what we found in Jesus' own teaching: transmuted eschatology with an additional element of real eschatology; it is, however, not quite the same. There is a slight difference which prevents us from tracing back this Johannine tradition immediately to Jesus Himself. He never speaks of the judgment as some inward experience of man: to Him it is some future event. He often talks about entering into life, but never as done by the very act of believing in His word: to do so is a privilege granted by God or His Messiah in a future time. On the other side, the idea of a bodily resurrection of all mankind on the day of judgment, so common in late Jewish literature and not uncommon even in the Synoptic Gospels, belongs rather to that stratum of later eschatological additions which we recognised there in our first lecture.

Here we may stop our inquiry into the Johannine branch of Gospel-tradition. The two illustrations I ventured to give will be sufficient, I trust, to show the complicated nature of Johannine doctrines, and what I think to be the right way of dealing with them. There are different stratifications, as modern research (Wendt, Spitta, Bacon, Wellhausen, Ed. Schwartz) has made more and more conspicuous.[1] Beside some genuine sayings of the Lord, we have what may be called the Johannine tradition, resting largely upon original conceptions of Jesus, but transforming them in the direction of mysticism; and then we have some additional matter, in our case the real eschatology, which perhaps may be traced back to the author of the Fourth Gospel, as distinguished from St. John; it is, however, possible that it belongs to a later redaction, of which chap. xxi. gives ample proof.

The main Johannine stratum, with its characteristics of individualistic, ethical, inward transformation of the current Jewish eschatology, bears signs of close

[1] Cp. H. L. Jackson, *The Fourth Gospel*, 1908.

affinity to the gospel of Jesus; but at the same time there is a marked difference: the Johannine doctrine has a distinct touch of mysticism, which is entirely wanting in the teaching of Jesus, and is to be explained by Hellenistic influences.

The validity of this distinction being granted, we may, without fear of misunderstanding, declare that we take the Johannine doctrine as an approximately good expression of Jesus' own views. The mystical inwardness of St. John certainly approaches far more nearly to Jesus' real meaning than the enlarging and enforcing of His eschatological utterances which we remarked in some passages of the Synoptic Gospels, especially St. Matthew. However strong Jesus' belief in eschatology might have been, it was only of secondary importance for His religious life, and for His teaching. It was a misunderstanding on the part of primitive Christianity when they laid the greatest stress on this side of the gospel. It may be called even a sign of decline that the expectation of some outward, realistic event overgrew the joyful experience of inward, present salvation. Later Christianity, when following the Johannine line of thought, came nearer to the true intention of Jesus Himself, notwithstanding His own belief in realistic eschatology.

Christianity is—and will ever be—the religion of sure salvation, brought by Jesus and to be experienced by His believers already during their present life. This does not exclude Christian hope. On the contrary, the more present salvation is experienced in mankind, the stronger Christian hope will be. This is the great lesson given to us by Jesus

Himself; He realised in Himself the complete and supreme communion with God, and yet He looked forward to a time of final salvation. He was the Son of God, and He had to bring salvation; but His gospel reached only few, and only individuals realised what was given to them in Jesus! However fully they submitted their own will to God, there were powers of evil outside them. The kingdom of God is not established so long as its dominion is only recognised by individuals; it wants to be collective, universal. Jesus' victory over Satan, His casting out of devils, was only an anticipation.

And this is the abiding truth in eschatology: it is to be sought not in the particulars of Jesus' coming and similar details, but in the fact that we have to expect and to pray for a state of things in which God's dominion will be fully established, and all obstacles, all evil energies finally destroyed.[1] We have seen in St. John's Gospel—and the later history of Christianity affords plenty of similar examples—that this looking out for some external real change is well combined with the finest and best inwardness. The Christian is a new creature, but he looks for a new heaven and a new earth, and his prayer will be for ever as His Lord taught him: "*Thy kingdom come.*"

[1] Cp. Dr. Kölbing (formerly Principal of the Moravian Seminary at Gnadenfeld): *Die bleibende Bedeutung der urchristlichen Eschatologie*, 1907.

www.ingramcontent.com/pod-product-compliance
Lightning Source LLC
La Vergne TN
LVHW010931100826
845153LV00001B/1

* 9 7 8 1 7 2 5 2 8 9 9 8 7 *